CONSCIOUS SYNERGY

The Evolution of Collective Consciousness

CONSCIOUS SYNERGY

The Evolution of Collective Consciousness

Conscious Synergy Movement

Copyright © 2026 by Conscious Synergy Movement
All rights reserved. No part of this book may be reproduced, stored in a retrieval system, or transmitted in any form or by any means—electronic, mechanical, photocopying, recording, or otherwise—without prior written permission from the publisher.

Published by
Conscious Synergy Movement
https://ConsciousSynergyMovement.com

ISBN: 979-8-218-92487-4

Printed in the United States of America.

Interior design by Conscious Synergy Movement
Palatino Linotype Typeface Family

First Edition, 2026

Dedication

To the One within all beings,
whose silent presence makes this work possible.

"Consciousness evolves through coherence,
and coherence begins within."
— *Conscious Synergy Movement*

TABLE OF CONTENTS

Preface — Orientation & Integration

There are moments in a lifetime when the interior landscape reorganizes itself—quietly, decisively—long before the outer world catches up. This book emerged from such a threshold. It was not written in a single arc, but assembled across years of inquiry, lived experience, energetic insight, and a deepening understanding of what it means to participate consciously in a universe woven from relationship.

Conscious Synergy is not a theory invented; it is a pattern remembered. Its essence is ancient, yet its articulation is new—rooted in science, shaped through psychology, and illuminated by the lived wisdom of human transformation. It speaks to the reality that coherence is not merely a personal state, but an evolutionary force, and that each of us carries a role in the unfolding of collective consciousness.

I offer this work as a bridge: between domains of knowledge, between inner experience and outer systems, between individual awakening and the possibility of a harmonized world. It was written with the intention that each chapter serve not only as information, but as activation—clarifying, awakening, and inviting the reader to inhabit their deepest resonance.

May this text support those who feel called toward truth, coherence, and a world aligned with the higher possibilities of our shared human journey.

For readers seeking a clear account of how empirical research, theoretical models, and experiential insight are integrated throughout this work, see "A Note on Sources and Integration.

A Note on Sources and Integration

This book weaves together established research, interdisciplinary theory, and experiential insight. Where claims align with peer-reviewed science—such as neuroscience, psychology, systems theory, and biofield research—they are grounded accordingly. Where the work draws from exploratory models, phenomenological frameworks, or influential thinkers whose contributions are interpretive rather than empirical, these are offered transparently as lenses for meaning-making rather than as settled science.

How to Use This Book

Pathway Guide: How to Enter This Work

This book is not meant to be rushed, mastered, or consumed in a single linear pass.

It was written to be inhabited.

The ideas here are layered, relational, and experiential. Some chapters may feel immediately familiar; others may feel disorienting, dense, or emotionally activating. This is not a sign that you are doing anything wrong. It is a sign that the material is working at more than one level at once.

You are invited to move through this book in the way that best supports your body, mind, and inner rhythm.

There is no correct order.
There is no test at the end.
There is no requirement to agree with everything you encounter.

Let this book meet you where you are.

How to Read This Book

You may read slowly or quickly.
You may pause often or move through entire chapters in one sitting.
You may reread a single paragraph for weeks and skip entire sections until later.

This work does not ask for belief.
It asks for presence.

If you notice moments of resistance, fatigue, emotional stirring, or confusion, consider that your system may be integrating rather than rejecting. Gentle pacing is not avoidance; it is regulation.

If at any point the material feels overwhelming, it is appropriate to stop, ground, breathe, and return later—or not at all. Coherence cannot be forced.

Suggested Reading Paths

These pathways are offered as orientation, not instruction. You may follow one, combine several, or ignore them entirely.

1. Healing-First Path

For readers focused on personal integration, trauma awareness, and inner coherence.
Recommended entry points:

- Movement I — Awaken
- Chapters on integrity, perception, regulation, and compassion
- Living Lexicon as companion
- This path emphasizes nervous system safety, self-understanding, and internal stabilization before outward action.

2. Leadership-First Path

For readers navigating responsibility, influence, decision-making, or group dynamics.

Recommended entry points:

- Movement II — Align
- Movement III — Activate
- Chapters on integrity, compassion, leadership, and collective evolution
- This path emphasizes regulated leadership, ethical clarity, and coherence in complex systems.

3. Systems-First Path

For readers drawn to theory, structure, and collective dynamics.
Recommended entry points:

- Chapters on systems, networks, the noosphere, and collective fields
- Visual Appendix
- Living Lexicon
- This path emphasizes pattern recognition, emergence, and relational intelligence across scales.

4. Technology and Future-Facing Path

For readers interested in AI, digital culture, and humanity's evolutionary trajectory.

Recommended entry points:

- Chapters on conscious technology, networks of consciousness, and the Future Human
- Visual Appendix
- Lexicon entries on coherence, noosphere, and synergy
- This path emphasizes ethical design, digital presence, and planetary participation.

About the Language in This Book

Some terms in this book—such as noosphere, biofield, coherence, metacognition, and synergy—carry layered meanings. They are used intentionally, but not rigidly.

You are not expected to fully understand every term on first encounter.
Definitions deepen through context.
Understanding unfolds through experience.

The Living Lexicon exists to support clarity without interrupting flow. (See Appendix D: Living Lexicon) It is a companion, not a requirement.

A Note on Depth and Safety

This book engages material that touches trauma, identity, belief systems, power, and collective wounds. It does so from a place of integration rather than pathologizing.

Still, if you notice emotional activation, dissociation, or distress beyond your capacity to regulate, it may be wise to pause and seek grounding or support. This work does not replace therapy, community, or care.

Self-honoring pacing is part of coherence.

Permission

You are permitted to:

Disagree
Question
Rest
Return later
Take what resonates
Leave what does not

You do not need to become anything to read this book.

A Final Orientation

This work is not asking you to transcend yourself.
It is inviting you to listen more closely to what is already present.

This book does not offer answers to memorize.
It offers lenses through which perception may soften, clarify, and reorganize.

If something here helps you feel more whole, more regulated, more truthful, or
more connected—to yourself, to others, or to the world—then it is doing its work.

Begin wherever you are.

Introduction

We live in a time when the structures that once defined meaning are dissolving. Institutions strain under the weight of their own fractures; cultural narratives grow thin; and many find themselves caught between the comfort of familiarity and the pull of an emerging future.

Something in us knows the old world cannot hold what is being born.

Across psychology, neuroscience, quantum theory, biofield research, leadership studies, and contemplative traditions, a converging truth is emerging: consciousness is relational.
Our thoughts, emotions, identities, and choices do not arise in isolation but within an energetic field shaped by our histories, environments, and shared humanity.

This book introduces Relational Synergy Theory (RST), developed within the Conscious Synergy Movement—an integrative framework that explores consciousness not as an isolated phenomenon, but as a dynamic, evolving residence within a larger field.

You will encounter three movements:

Movement I — Awaken
Reveals the vibrational nature of consciousness and the human biofield.

Movement II — Align
Explores the architecture of identity, relationship, coherence, and psychological healing.

Movement III — Activate
Integrates technology, leadership, and the emerging future of human consciousness.

Together, these movements map a path for becoming synergy—an embodied expression of coherence that supports the evolution of the collective field.

This book is not merely to be read; it is to be entered. Let it be a mirror, a companion, and a catalyst for remembering the deeper intelligence that animates all life.

Orientation Line

This introduction situates Conscious Synergy as an integrative framework—
preparing the reader to move beyond isolated selfhood and into a relational
understanding of consciousness, coherence, and collective evolution.

Scholarly Context

The integrative perspective presented in this introduction is informed by
converging work across multiple disciplines, including developmental
psychology and systems theory (Wilber; Corning), neuroscience and embodied
cognition (Siegel; Damasio), biofield and coherence research (Oschman;
McCraty), consciousness studies and field-based models (Laszlo), and
contemplative science bridging subjective and intersubjective awareness (Varela).
Together, these bodies of work reflect a growing recognition of consciousness as
relational, embedded, and co-emergent rather than isolated or purely individual.

SKEPTICISM & SCIENTIFIC GROUNDING

Human development has always lived at the intersection of what can be measured and what can only be experienced. This book draws from both. Throughout the chapters ahead, terms such as field, biofield, coherence, and resonance are used in ways that bridge emerging science, psychology, and lived human experience.

A few clarifications may support your reading:

1. "Field" is not a metaphor.
In this framework, the field refers to the dynamic interplay of physiological, emotional, cognitive, and relational information that shapes perception and behavior. This includes measurable processes—such as bioelectromagnetic activity, autonomic regulation, and heart–brain rhythms—as well as subtle phenomena documented in biofield and interpersonal neurobiology research.

2. This book does not claim final answers.
The science of consciousness is evolving. Where empirical evidence exists, it is referenced. Where lived experience extends beyond current measurement, it is named without overstatement.

3. Healthy skepticism is welcome here.
Skepticism, in its truest form, is curiosity with boundaries. You do not need to accept every concept immediately. Hold each idea lightly and test it against your experience. Notice what resonates, what challenges you, and what expands possibility.

4. Conscious Synergy is a framework, not a doctrine.
It is offered as a developmental lens—integrating trauma psychology, systems theory, energy science, and the reality of lived human transformation. Readers are invited into exploration, not belief.

Hold these ideas the way you hold your own awakening—gently, intentionally, and with a willingness to see what reveals itself.

KEY CONCEPTS AT A GLANCE

An Orientation Map for the Journey Ahead

HOW TO USE THIS PAGE

This page is not meant to be memorized.
It is a reference compass—something you may return to as concepts deepen through experience.

CORE FRAMEWORK

Conscious Synergy

A framework for understanding how individual awareness, nervous system regulation, relational integrity, and collective systems interact to shape human experience and social evolution.
Conscious Synergy emphasizes coherence, conscious participation, and the inseparability of personal healing and collective transformation.

Relational Synergy Theory (RST)

The theoretical backbone of Conscious Synergy.

RST views consciousness as relational rather than isolated, emerging through interaction within human, social, and energetic fields. Identity, meaning, and behavior are shaped not in isolation—but in relationship.

DEVELOPMENTAL MAP

Character · Player · Developer

A developmental role map describing how individuals relate to self, others, and systems:

- **<u>Character</u>**
  Operates primarily from conditioning and survival patterns.
  Life feels reactive; conflict is often experienced as threat.
- **<u>Player</u>**
  Gains awareness and agency within existing systems.
  Begins to recognize patterns, regulate responses, and make conscious choices.
- **<u>Developer</u>**
  Perceives system dynamics and acts to redesign patterns with integrity and coherence.
  Operates from alignment rather than control.

FOUNDATIONAL STATES

Coherence

A state of internal alignment across physiological, emotional, cognitive, and relational systems.
Coherence supports clarity, resilience, ethical action, and the capacity to remain present without fragmentation.

Integrity

Coherence expressed as action.
Integrity is alignment between inner truth and outer behavior—not moral
perfection, but structural wholeness.

Compassion

A regulated state of presence that allows openness without self-abandonment.
Compassion arises when awareness, integrity, and nervous system safety
converge.

FIELD CONCEPTS

Field / Relational Field

The dynamic context in which perception, emotion, behavior, and meaning arise.
Includes both measurable physiological and relational processes and experiential
patterns influencing human interaction.

Biofield

The organizing field of biological, electromagnetic, and informational processes
that regulate human functioning.
Referenced here as an emerging scientific domain and experiential model, not
settled doctrine.

Noosphere

The collective layer of human thought, meaning, and cultural patterning.
In this framework, the noosphere reflects how individual coherence or distortion
scales into collective systems.

EMERGENT DYNAMICS

Synergy

An emergent quality that arises when individuals and systems interact in ways
that increase collective capacity, intelligence, and resilience.
Synergy cannot be forced—it emerges through alignment, trust, and coherence.

MOVEMENT I — AWAKEN

*Where consciousness begins to remember itself
and the quiet architecture of frequency comes alive.*

MOVEMENT I — AWAKEN

CHAPTER 1

THE FOUNDATIONS OF CONSCIOUS SYNERGY

Poetic Insight

There is a rhythm beneath the visible world—a quiet pulse moving through atoms and bodies, memory and meaning, through the ache of becoming and the luminosity of awakening.

We sense it before we can explain it. Something within us recognizes the pattern: the gradual movement from fragmentation toward wholeness, from survival toward coherence, from isolation toward a deeper field of belonging.

This is consciousness evolving through us.

And when the individual begins to feel this rhythm—not as noise, but as signal—a new possibility opens.

A possibility called synergy.

Chapter Summary

This chapter establishes the foundations of Conscious Synergy as both an inner developmental process and an emergent pattern within human evolution. Drawing from psychology, consciousness studies, energy systems, and Hawkins' Map of Consciousness, it introduces consciousness as a field of frequency and information, explores how identity organizes in response to that field, and presents the Conscious Role Map—Character, Player, Developer—as a practical lens for transformation.

Synergy is framed not as an abstract ideal, but as a living developmental threshold: the point at which coherence becomes more compelling than survival strategies, and reactive existence begins to give way to intentional embodiment. This chapter lays the groundwork for the entire book by clarifying the forces, patterns, and principles that shape human awakening and collective evolution.

Role Windows

Throughout this book, you will encounter Role Windows—brief experiential snapshots that illuminate how consciousness organizes itself at different stages of development. These roles are not fixed identities but evolving positions of perception, regulation, and agency. As the book unfolds, the Role Windows will deepen and shift, reflecting the reader's movement through awareness rather than explaining it outright.

ROLE WINDOW

The Request — Unconscious Role

The request arrives without warning, though something in them recognizes the familiar tightening before the words are fully formed. It sounds reasonable. Necessary, even. Others are already nodding.

They agree quickly, almost reflexively, before checking what it will cost. Saying no feels dangerous—like withdrawing from belonging, like risking disapproval they may not survive. The body goes quiet, bracing. The decision is already made.

Later, unease settles in. Fatigue follows. Resentment simmers without a clear target. They replay the moment, wondering when things went wrong, unsure how a simple yes became a private burden.

They don't yet recognize this as a boundary crossed. It feels more like a personal failure—another instance of not being enough, or being too much, or somehow missing the right response.

The system moves on.
They absorb the weight.

1. Consciousness as the Field of Becoming

Human transformation does not begin with behavior. It begins earlier—at the level of perception, in the subtle ways reality is interpreted before thought finds language. Beneath every reaction sits an assumption. Beneath every assumption, a state. And beneath every state lies an organizing field—one that quietly shapes what we notice, what we ignore, what we brace for, and what we allow to be true.

Every experience unfolds within a broader field of consciousness—a living tapestry of signals, patterns, and possibilities. Across modern consciousness research, contemplative traditions, and emerging biofield science, a shared insight appears: consciousness may not be merely a byproduct of the brain, but a participatory substrate within which the brain operates.

In this view, consciousness is not simply something we possess.
It is something we are continually becoming.

Each person inhabits an internal landscape shaped by developmental imprinting, belief systems, nervous system conditioning, relational history, trauma and resilience, cultural programming, and the unique signature of awareness itself. These forces do not merely color experience; they organize it. They determine what feels safe, what feels threatening, what appears possible, and what disappears from awareness altogether.

This is why two people standing in the same moment can inhabit entirely different worlds. Their nervous systems read different signals. Their histories activate different interpretations. Their inner fields generate different meaning.

This variability is not random. It follows recognizable patterns. Hawkins' Map of Consciousness—while not empirical in the conventional scientific sense—articulates something many have directly perceived: states of consciousness organize perception. Shame configures reality differently than courage. Fear filters experience differently than love. Coherence reveals a world unlike fragmentation. Readers may also choose to engage with this map symbolically rather than as measurement, using it as a phenomenologically resonant lens rather than a scientific scale.

When perceptual structures shift, identity reorganizes. And when identity reorganizes, behavior follows—not through force or discipline, but through internal alignment.

The foundation of conscious evolution, then, is not effort.
It is coherence.

Emerging biofield research, quantum biological models, and subtle-energy traditions across cultures converge on a related understanding: the human system functions as an electromagnetic and informational field in constant dialogue with its environment. We sense life not only through cognition, but through resonance. We absorb signal, generate signal, interpret signal, and respond to subtle frequencies—shaping, and being shaped by, the relational field we inhabit.

This is why personal evolution cannot be reduced to psychology alone. It is energetic as well. As internal coherence strengthens, perception clarifies. Reactivity softens. Compassion becomes accessible. Truth-tolerance expands. Intuition refines. Discernment sharpens. The self becomes less governed by protection and more capable of presence.

These qualities form the living ground of Conscious Synergy.

Bridging the Gap: Consciousness as Experience, Not Abstraction

In an age shaped by data and metrics, conversations about consciousness can feel slippery—too philosophical, insufficiently grounded, or suspiciously mystical.

This resistance is not accidental. Dominant cultural frameworks often treat subjective experience as secondary: an echo of biology rather than the field in which biology operates. Consciousness is pushed to the margins, framed as effect rather than medium.

Yet lived experience quietly contradicts this view.

Recall a moment when a shift in your internal state—from anxiety to calm, resentment to clarity, or confusion to conviction—changed your experience of the world before any external circumstance moved. Perception transformed first. Reality reorganized second.

In this book, consciousness is not presented as speculation. It is treated as the foundational medium of human experience: the living architecture that determines what we notice, how we interpret it, and what we believe is possible.

To study consciousness is not to abandon rigor.
It is to apply rigor to the ground from which all observation arises.

How States Organize Reality: A Contrast in Perception

Consider the same moment, lived from two different internal states.

A person receives critical feedback about their work.

In a contracted state—colored by fear or shame—the feedback registers as threat. The nervous system tightens. Attention narrows. Meaning collapses toward self-protection.

They don't respect me.
I'm failing.
I need to defend myself or shut down.

The words are identical.
The interpretation is not.

Now imagine the same moment arising from a coherent state—grounded, present, regulated. The body remains open. The feedback lands without collapse. Curiosity replaces threat.

Is there something here I can learn from?
What truth can I take in without diminishing myself?

Nothing external has changed.
What has shifted is the state of consciousness from which perception arises.

This is not positive thinking or moral superiority. It is state-dependent perception—a phenomenon observed across psychology, neuroscience, contemplative traditions, and lived human experience.

Conscious Synergy begins here: not with control over circumstances, but with awareness of the internal field shaping how reality is perceived and engaged.

2. Conscious Synergy as an Evolutionary Pattern

Synergy is not metaphorical. It is a pattern observable across living systems. In nature, synergy appears when individual units interact in ways that generate outcomes impossible in isolation—cells forming organs, mycelial networks sustaining forests, bees functioning as a hive, humans collaborating with shared intention.

When relationship becomes coherent, a higher-order function emerges.

Conscious Synergy names something more precise: the evolutionary capacity of an individual to move from fragmented survival patterns into coherent, relational, purpose-aligned states of being. It is synergy made conscious—embodied in identity, ethics, and presence.

Human consciousness evolves through identifiable thresholds. Life often begins in unconscious survival, shaped by inherited strategies and reactive patterning. Awakening follows—sometimes through suffering, sometimes through longing, sometimes through sudden clarity—when perception is revealed as mutable rather than fixed.

Alignment becomes possible when coherence is intentionally cultivated through emotional integration, nervous-system healing, perceptual refinement, and integrity development.

Synergy emerges when these shifts stabilize into a way of being—when coherence becomes baseline and relationship becomes a place where presence can remain intact. From synergy flows embodied contribution: the expression of one's unique frequency in service to the whole.

This matters now because the forces shaping humanity—technological acceleration, ecological strain, global interdependence, ideological fragmentation—are not merely sociopolitical. They are evolutionary pressures.

Complexity requires more than intelligence.
It requires integration.

Conscious Synergy is not only personal transformation.
It is the adaptive response of a species entering a new developmental stage.

3. The Conscious Role Map: Character → Player → Developer

To understand how individuals evolve into synergy, we need a map—not a rigid

Conscious Role Map

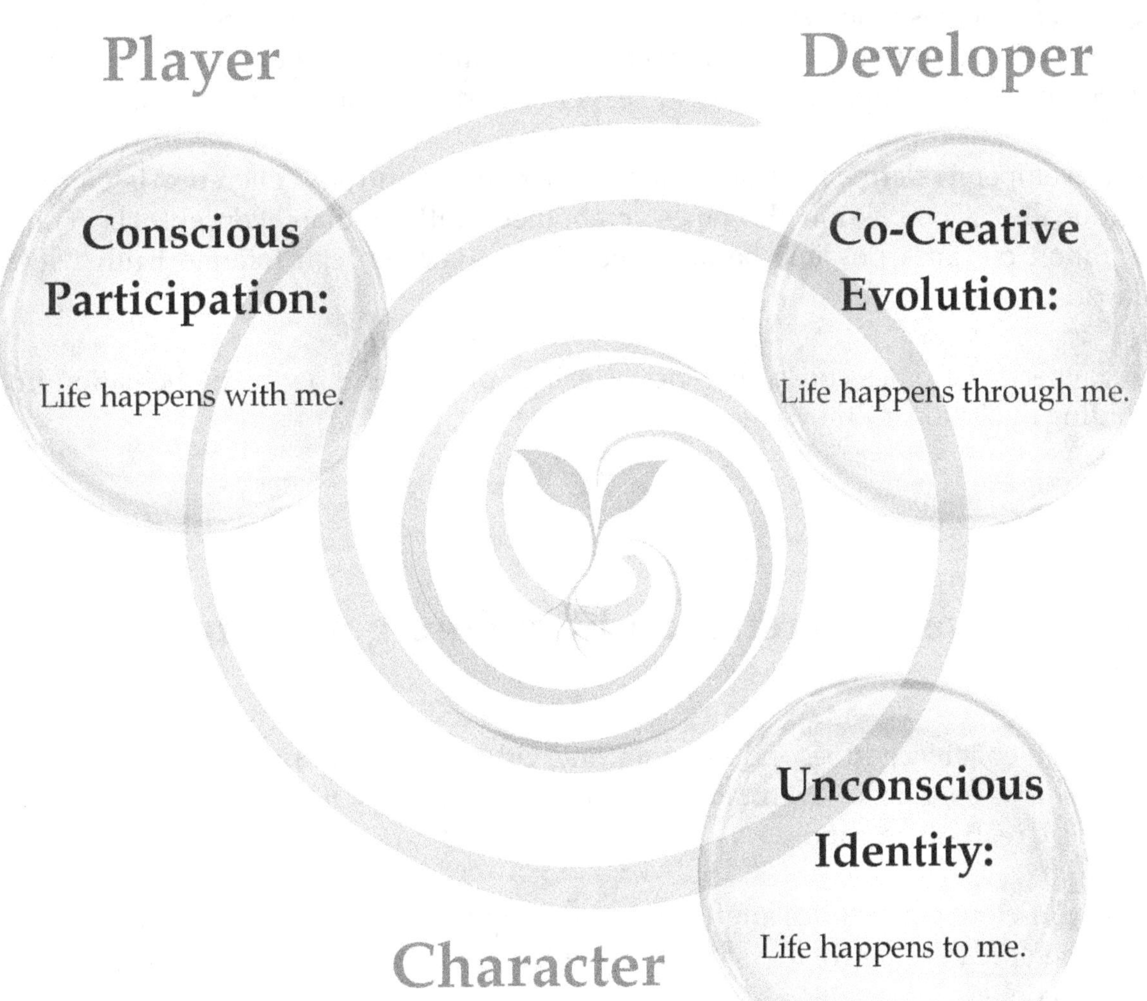

Figure V.1 — The Conscious Role Map represents three developmental orientations of human consciousness. These roles are not hierarchical identities but states we shift through as awareness deepens. Synergy emerges as we move from reactive participation to intentional co-creation.

typology or spiritual hierarchy, but a fluid developmental arc that honors human complexity. The Conscious Role Map offers such a structure: Character, Player, Developer. (See Figure V.1)

The Character is identity organized around inherited patterning—family systems, cultural conditioning, trauma imprinting, internalized narratives, and fear-based interpretation. Life often feels like something happening to the individual. The Character is not wrong or inferior; it is unexamined.

The Player emerges when awareness awakens enough to question the script. Reactions are noticed. Narratives are examined. Inner authority begins to form. This is metacognition—the capacity to observe experience rather than be ruled by it.

The Developer is defined by alignment rather than control. Coherence is cultivated intentionally. Compassion becomes embodied rather than conceptual. Trauma integration becomes possible because the nervous system can tolerate truth without collapse.

Here, synergy becomes conscious—not as self-improvement, but as participation in an unfolding evolutionary movement.

4. Collective Coherence and the Emergent Future

Individual coherence does not remain individual. As internal stability increases, relationships reorganize. Communication becomes less reactive. Truth becomes more tolerable. Creativity expands.

Across consciousness studies and lived human experience, a consistent insight appears: coherence spreads. Nervous systems co-regulate. Emotional states propagate through relational fields.

When enough individuals cross the threshold from reactivity to synergy, collective systems begin to reorganize.

The Conscious Synergy Movement arises from this understanding: personal evolution and collective evolution are inseparable. Conscious Synergy offers a framework for participating in that reorganization with intention rather than fear.

5. The Path Beyond Separation

Every human carries a story of fragmentation—loss, trauma, misattunement, shame, and survival strategies formed in response to threat. These wounds do not signal failure. They mark the moment consciousness begins to recognize itself.

Healing is not denial of pain.
It is the capacity to hold pain without being reorganized by it.

Synergy is the moment consciousness remembers itself—not as an isolated unit, but as part of a living field.

Closing Reflection

There comes a point when the old story can no longer carry the weight of who we are becoming—when survival yields to presence, fragmentation gives way to coherence, and identity expands enough to breathe.

This chapter has laid the foundation for understanding Conscious Synergy not as philosophy, but as an unfolding evolutionary pattern.

Between who we have been and who we are becoming lies a threshold.

Synergy begins there.

Synergy in Practice — Micro-Practice

- Pause and bring attention to your body.
- Without changing anything, notice where you feel settled and where you feel tense or fragmented.
- Name the automatic pattern.
- Gently ask yourself: Where in my life am I responding automatically rather than consciously?
- Resist the urge to fix.
- Do not analyze or correct the response. Allow awareness to replace urgency.
- Stay with presence.
- Notice what shifts when attention becomes kind, curious, and grounded.

Coherence begins the moment awareness replaces reactivity.

Orientation Line

This chapter invites the reader to recognize coherence not as an ideal to strive for, but as a natural state that becomes accessible when awareness replaces reactivity.

Scholarly Context

The conceptual foundations of this chapter draw from integrative work across consciousness studies, neuroscience, developmental psychology, systems theory, and biofield research. Key influences include phenomenological and developmental models of consciousness (Wilber), interpersonal neurobiology and embodied cognition (Siegel; Damasio), trauma-informed understandings of nervous-system organization (van der Kolk; Porges), coherence and biofield research (Oschman; McCraty), systems emergence (Corning), and phenomenological approaches to participatory awareness (Varela). Hawkins' Map of Consciousness is included as a non-empirical but phenomenologically resonant framework describing how states of awareness organize perception and behavior.

MOVEMENT I — AWAKEN

CHAPTER 2

THE ARCHITECTURE OF AWARENESS

Poetic Insight

Now we step inside the mechanics of awareness itself.

Awareness is the first light—the quiet illumination that reveals the shape of our inner world before we attempt to change it.

It is the mirror that shows us not only who we believe we are, but the deeper patterns moving beneath thought, beneath noise, beneath the practiced self we learned to wear.

Awareness is both witness and sculptor, shaping identity by revealing what has always been present.

It is here, in this luminous interior, that the journey of Conscious Synergy truly begins.

Chapter Summary

This chapter explores awareness as the primary architecture of human consciousness. It examines the inner mechanisms that shape perception—cognitive, emotional, energetic, and relational—and how these mechanisms determine the pathways available to an individual's evolution. Drawing from psychology, metacognition, biofield science, and contemplative traditions, the chapter maps how awareness develops, how it becomes distorted, and how it can be refined into the coherent perceptual system required for synergy.

The chapter explores core structures of human experience: how the Perception Loop forms, how the Narrative Self stabilizes identity, how the emotional body and nervous system shape interpretation, how energetic and relational fields influence what is sensed, and how the metacognitive witness becomes the stabilizing center of transformation.

This chapter prepares the evolutionary arc in Chapter 3 by clarifying how humans experience reality from the inside out—and how expanded awareness transforms every domain of life.

1. Awareness as the First Technology of Consciousness

Before tools, language, culture, or systems, humanity possessed one fundamental instrument: awareness. It is easy to treat awareness as obvious—something we "just have"—but awareness is not merely the ability to notice. It is the living interface between consciousness and experience: a system that interprets, organizes, filters, and assigns meaning. It does not simply receive reality. It shapes reality by determining what becomes foreground and what remains unseen.

Modern psychology, neuroscience, and contemplative science converge on a central point: we do not respond to reality itself. We respond to our perception of reality. This distinction changes everything. If perception is shaped by internal architecture, then transformation begins by illuminating that architecture.

Awareness is not passive. It is creative. It assigns relevance, filters information, and constructs the world we believe we inhabit. This makes awareness the primary blueprint from which most human experience emerges—not because awareness is "the answer," but because awareness determines what is even available to be answered.

2. The Perception Loop: How Reality Is Constructed

Each person lives inside a perceptual loop: a feedback system through which stimuli become meaning, meaning becomes response, and response reinforces an internal model of what is "real." The loop begins with sensation—sensory, emotional, intuitive, or energetic input. That input is filtered through beliefs, memory, trauma imprinting, cultural conditioning, and relational history. Interpretation follows, and meaning forms: the mind's story about what the input signifies. (See Figure V.2)

From there the body responds—behaviorally, emotionally, physiologically, or relationally. Then reinforcement arrives: outcomes confirm or adjust the internal model, slowly building identity through repetition. Over time, the loop becomes self-confirming. It does not merely describe reality. It becomes the lens through which reality is encountered.

Most of this occurs beneath conscious awareness. By adulthood, much perception is automated. This is why awakening often feels like disruption: the unsettling realization that what we assumed was fixed was actually interpreted. The world may not have changed—the lens has simply been revealed.

THE PERCEPTION LOOP

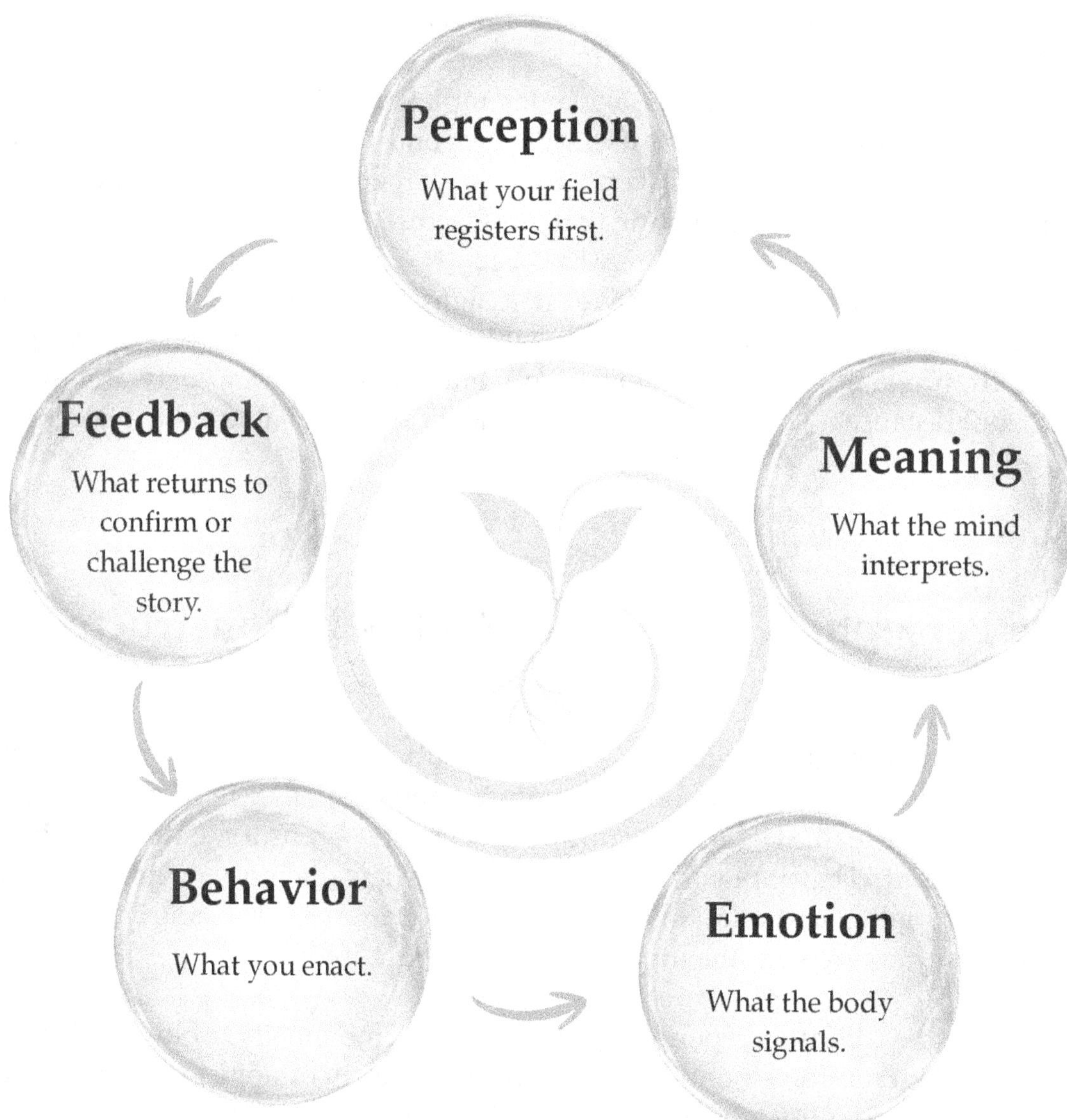

Figure V.2 — The Perception Loop
A recurring feedback system through which perception, meaning, emotion, behavior, and outcome reinforce one another until awareness intervenes.

When awareness enters the loop, the loop can evolve.
Without awareness, it repeats.

Consider a familiar moment: a message goes unanswered longer than expected.

The stimulus is simple—silence. But silence rarely arrives empty. It enters a loop already shaped by attachment history, nervous system state, and learned expectation. For one person, the delay registers as neutral. For another, it triggers anxiety. The body tightens. Meaning forms quickly. Emotion follows. Behavior organizes itself around protection.

The loop completes when the outcome reinforces the assumption. Distance confirms rejection. Anxiety confirms unworthiness. The story hardens.

Yet nothing objective has been revealed—only the internal architecture through which the stimulus was interpreted.

A Lived Moment of Awareness

It happens quietly.

A message arrives later than expected. Nothing explicit is said, yet something tightens inside. Attention narrows. The body registers the shift before the mind explains it.

Breath shortens slightly. The chest firms. A familiar alertness spreads—subtle, practiced, insistent. The nervous system prepares for a threat that has not yet been confirmed.

Then awareness arrives—without force.

The sensation is noticed before the story finishes itself. The interpretation forming is recognized as familiar rather than factual. No conclusion is drawn. No reaction is rushed.

The body is allowed to feel without urgency.

In that pause, the loop loosens. Meaning becomes provisional instead of absolute. The system stays present rather than reorganizing around assumption.

Nothing has changed externally.

The lens has.

This is how perception becomes visible—not through analysis, but through awareness that remains long enough for the architecture to reveal itself.

Trauma and the Distortion of Perception

Trauma does not only leave emotional residue. It alters the loop itself. The nervous system becomes sensitized, meaning narrows, assumptions skew toward threat, and the past begins to overwrite the present. Neutral cues can register as danger. Silence can feel like rejection. Boundaries can feel like abandonment. This distortion is not a flaw. It is adaptation—protection shaped by lived experience.

But when adaptation becomes identity, the individual becomes trapped in inherited scripts rather than emergent possibility.

Awareness Collapse and Awareness Expansion

Under threat, awareness collapses toward immediacy. Attention fixes on danger. Time compresses. Options narrow. This is not failure—it is survival intelligence.

Consider a heated argument or exposure to alarming news headlines. The nervous system activates. Attention locks onto threat cues. Nuance disappears. The body prepares for defense. Meaning collapses into urgency: Something is wrong. I must react now.

Awareness expands when regulation allows perception to widen. Context returns. The present becomes distinguishable from the past. Sensation can be felt without overwhelming the system.

In the same situation—news, conflict, disagreement—expanded awareness allows the system to pause. The body remains present. Multiple interpretations become possible. Response replaces reaction.

Expansion does not erase pain.
It allows pain without letting it monopolize meaning.

Synergy depends on this flexibility. Awareness cannot be forced open. It expands as safety, coherence, and regulation increase.

Awareness is the capacity to see the loop rather than unconsciously live inside it.

That shift marks the beginning of liberation.

3. The Narrative Self and the Illusion of Continuity

Human identity is assembled through narrative. We make sense of our lives by telling stories about who we are, what has happened, what is possible, and what is forbidden. These stories become scaffolding: they stabilize the self, reduce uncertainty, and create continuity across time.

Yet the narrative self is not fixed. It is a cognitive construction—flexible, malleable, and profoundly influenced by emotion, memory, culture, and belief. The story we tell is not merely description. It is interpretive architecture that shapes what we notice, what we fear, and what we expect.

When narrative becomes rigid, identity becomes rigid. A person who believes "I am unworthy," "I am broken," "Nothing ever changes," "I cannot trust," "I must not fail," or "This is just who I am" will filter life through those constructs. The narrative becomes a perceptual prison—not by intention, but by repetition.

But when narrative becomes conscious—when we recognize the story is occurring within awareness rather than defining awareness—the architecture of identity begins to shift. The self becomes capable of authoring rather than only reenacting. This is one of the earliest thresholds of synergy: when the story no longer governs the self, and the self can hold the story without being governed by it.

4. The Nervous System and Emotional Body: The Felt Architecture

Awareness is not purely cognitive. It is embodied. The nervous system shapes our capacity to remain present, regulate emotion, interpret threat accurately, connect with others, tolerate truth, and access higher states of consciousness. The nervous system is not background machinery—it is part of the architecture of awareness.

The emotional body signals whether the internal environment is coherent or distressed. Emotion is not merely "feeling." It is information—movement—energy shaping readiness, perception, and meaning-making. When this system is regulated, awareness becomes more spacious. When it is dysregulated, awareness narrows.

State determines perception. A regulated system tends to perceive possibility. A dysregulated system tends to perceive threat. This is why emotional healing is not merely therapeutic. It is perceptual evolution. As the nervous system stabilizes, interpretation becomes more accurate, identity becomes more fluid, and synergy becomes more accessible.

In this way, awareness cannot be refined through insight alone. It must be refined through the body's capacity to remain present with what is true.

5. The Energetic Field: Awareness Beyond the Brain

Emerging biofield science and subtle energy traditions point toward an expanded understanding of awareness: awareness may extend beyond cognition. The human energy field appears to store information, transmit and receive signal, interact with relational fields, reflect emotional and psychological states, and influence subtle perception.

The biofield functions as both filter and amplifier. When the field is fragmented, perception becomes unstable—intuition becomes noisy, relational signal becomes confusing, and inner experience can feel disjointed. When the field is coherent, perception tends to clarify. This is one reason synergy is ultimately an energetic state: a frequency of awareness in which disparate parts of the self move into alignment.

Awareness, from this view, is not limited to thought. It is an interface between nervous system, energy field, environment, and relational signal. As coherence increases, perception becomes more reliable—not as perfection, but as improved signal-to-noise.

6. The Relational Field: Awareness as Interconnection

Human beings do not exist as isolated units. Awareness is profoundly relational. The relational field includes family systems, cultural narratives, social identities, emotional resonance with others, energetic exchange, and collective consciousness structures. We learn ourselves through others long before we learn ourselves within. Identity is formed inside relationship—which means awareness is shaped inside relationship.

This is why co-regulation matters. A calm presence can soothe another nervous system. An attuned relationship can soften trauma patterns. A coherent field can stabilize a distressed one. These are not sentimental claims; they are relational mechanics.

Synergy is not merely inner work. It is the mutual shaping of consciousness through connection—an emergent coherence that arises when awareness is held within resonance.

7. Metacognition: The Witness Within

At the core of conscious evolution is metacognition—the ability to observe thoughts, emotions, sensations, and patterns without merging with them. Metacognition is the inner witness. It allows the individual to interrupt automatic cycles, question assumptions, examine narratives, track emotional states, notice energetic shifts, and choose rather than react.

This capacity expands through practice and inquiry, but it is also a natural developmental threshold. As metacognition strengthens, a profound reorganization becomes possible: the self is no longer defined entirely by fear, impulse, inherited belief, trauma residue, or old scripts.

The witness becomes the architect of synergy because it provides stability for transformation. Without a witness, the system remains reactive. With a witness, the system gains choice—and choice is the doorway through which coherence enters.

8. Awareness as a Developmental Threshold

Awareness evolves through stages, each expanding what a person can perceive, hold, and integrate. Early awareness recognizes inner experience. More mature awareness perceives context, patterns, and influence. Meta-awareness observes perception itself. Energetic and relational awareness deepen as coherence grows. Systemic awareness recognizes larger structures and feedback loops. Noetic awareness begins to perceive consciousness as unified and participatory.

These thresholds are not achievements to display. They are expansions of capacity. Synergy becomes possible when these layers begin to unify—when awareness becomes not only a tool used occasionally, but a way of being that remains present across changing conditions.

9. Distortions, Blind Spots, and the Edges of Awareness

Every perceptual system contains blind spots. Awareness becomes limited when constrained by unresolved trauma, inflated ego, spiritual bypassing, over-identification with intellect, fear of truth, habit loops, cultural conditioning, attachment injuries, moral rigidity, or energetic depletion.

These distortions do not indicate failure. They indicate where consciousness is still evolving. They reveal the edges of what the system can currently hold.

Synergy requires the courage to meet these edges with honesty. Awareness grows when we stop protecting the illusion of who we think we are and begin listening to the deeper truth of who we are becoming.

The edges are not barriers.
They are doorways.

10. Awareness as the Foundation of Synergy

Awareness is the human capacity that can integrate thought, emotion, energy, intuition, memory, sensation, relational dynamics, and meaning. It is the organizing principle of the inner world. Without awareness, change is difficult because the system cannot see itself. With awareness, change becomes increasingly inevitable because awareness becomes the point of integration through which fragmented domains can be observed, related, and reorganized.

Without awareness, systems operate in isolation—physiological responses occur without reflection, thoughts arise without examination, and relational patterns repeat without interruption. Each domain functions, but not in coherence.

Awareness introduces a new capacity: the ability to perceive interaction itself.

It allows the individual to recognize not only what is happening within each domain, but how these domains influence one another—how emotion shapes cognition, how cognition directs behavior, how behavior reinforces relational dynamics, and how those dynamics feed back into identity.

This recursive perception is the beginning of regulation.

At the individual level, this appears as metacognition—the capacity to observe one's own thoughts, responses, and patterns. But when extended across relational systems, this same process becomes meta-regulation: the capacity of a system to observe, evaluate, and modify the rules by which it operates.

In this way, awareness is not passive. It is structurally generative.

It introduces flexibility where there was rigidity, interruption where there was automaticity, and possibility where there was repetition.

Without awareness, change depends on external force or disruption. With awareness, change becomes internally accessible.

This is why awareness is not simply a state of consciousness—it is a developmental threshold.

It marks the transition from participation within a system to participation in the shaping of that system.

As awareness deepens, coherence becomes possible—not because the system is controlled, but because it is understood.

Closing Reflection

Awareness is the inner terrain we must learn to navigate with precision, compassion, and honesty. It is the foundation upon which evolution rests.

When awareness becomes coherent, the self begins to reorganize. When the self reorganizes, the world becomes perceptible in new ways. And when perception changes, possibility expands—not as fantasy, but as lived capacity.

In the next chapter, we step back to view the larger arc: the evolution of human consciousness across time, culture, and the collective field. To know where we are going, we must understand how we arrived here.

The architecture of awareness is the doorway.
Synergy is what waits on the other side.

Synergy in Practice

Throughout the day, notice how different environments affect your internal state. Track shifts in energy when entering a room, engaging in conversation, or interacting online.

Rather than analyzing, simply register. Ask: What does my system sense before my mind interprets?

This practice strengthens sensitivity to the field without turning awareness into vigilance.

Orientation Line

This chapter establishes awareness as the foundational architecture of perception—preparing the reader to understand evolution not as abstraction, but as lived, embodied change.

Scholarly Context

The perspectives in this chapter draw upon integrative research and theory across psychology, neuroscience, consciousness studies, trauma-informed frameworks, and biofield science. Key influences include models of perception and meaning-making (Siegel; Damasio), metacognition and self-observation (Siegel; Varela), trauma and nervous system organization (van der Kolk; Porges; Lanius), systems and constructivist understandings of perception (Meadows), and emerging research on human biofields and coherence (Oschman; Jain & Mills). Together, these frameworks support an understanding of awareness as embodied, relational, and field-based rather than purely cognitive or internally isolated.

MOVEMENT I — AWAKEN

CHAPTER 3

THE ARC OF HUMAN EVOLUTION

Poetic Insight

Every life echoes an ancient story—of emergence, fracture, longing, and expansion—of consciousness learning to know itself through the fragile vessels of human experience.

What looks like an individual journey is part of a much older movement: a collective remembering. A gradual awakening of the species from instinct to awareness, from awareness to compassion, and from compassion to synergy.

We are not separate from this unfolding. We are its expression—its texture, its threshold, its living possibility.

Human evolution is not only biological. It is perceptual. Relational. Energetic. Conscious.

To understand where we are going, we must remember the path that brought us here.

Chapter Summary

This chapter situates Conscious Synergy within the broad sweep of human evolution, integrating insights from developmental psychology, anthropology, systems theory, consciousness studies, and emerging perspectives on collective fields. We explore how humanity's arc reflects increasing complexity, expanding awareness, and a gradual movement from survival-based consciousness toward relational, cooperative, and synergistic capacities.

We trace three interwoven layers of evolution—biological, psychological, and consciousness evolution—and examine how trauma, culture, and structural systems have interrupted or distorted this arc. We then explore the modern era as an unprecedented pressure-cooker of complexity, requiring a new mode of being.

Finally, we frame synergy as the next phase of human evolution: not merely personal transformation, but a collective developmental threshold.

ROLE WINDOW

The Request — Aware Role

The request arrives, and this time something pauses. The familiar tightening still appears, but it is noticed—not yet understood, just registered. There is a moment where the body speaks before the words are answered.

They still feel the pull to agree. The impulse is strong, practiced. But now it carries a faint signal beneath it—an awareness that this moment matters, that something is being asked beyond the task itself.

They nod more slowly. They hear themselves say yes, but the sound lands differently. A question lingers: Did I actually choose that? The unease does not wait until later this time. It walks alongside the decision.

Afterward, instead of only fatigue, there is curiosity. They replay the moment not to punish themselves, but to understand it. Awareness has entered the room. The pattern is no longer invisible.

1. Human Evolution as an Expansion of Awareness

Humanity's story is often told in the language of survival, conflict, and innovation. Those forces are real, yet beneath them runs a quieter current: the gradual expansion of consciousness. Across time, the human system has grown not only in capacity to endure, but in capacity to perceive—an increasing ability to take in more of reality, integrate it, and respond with greater nuance.

From early sensory awareness to symbolic language, from social bonding to moral reasoning, from mythic imagination to scientific inquiry, each shift reflects a widening aperture. The species has been learning how to hold more: more complexity, more ambiguity, more interdependence, more responsibility for impact.

Human evolution is not best understood as a ladder of "better" and "worse." It is more accurate to see it as an expansion of capacity—capacity to sense, to feel, to reflect, to connect, and to act with coherence. In this deeper sense, evolution is the gradual enlargement of what can be perceived and metabolized without collapse.

2. The Brain as the Instrument of Awareness

Across millennia, the human brain developed functions that support increasingly complex forms of consciousness: reflexive awareness, emotional depth, symbolic meaning-making, abstraction and imagination, planning and foresight, moral reasoning, self–other differentiation, and intuitive pattern detection. These capacities are not separate from spirituality or energy; they are biological correlates of expanding awareness—the living instrument through which perception becomes more refined.

Yet this is not a celebration of cognition alone. The nervous system is shaped by threat, belonging, attachment, and environment. As the brain evolved, it carried both brilliance and vulnerability. It can expand awareness—and it can organize awareness around fear. This is one reason progress looks paradoxical: technological sophistication can coexist with psychological fragmentation, and advanced intelligence can coexist with primitive reactivity.

An essential truth emerges here: higher awareness requires higher regulation. Greater perception requires greater coherence. Otherwise, complexity overwhelms the system and regression follows. Evolution is not only about what the mind can compute; it is also about what the body can tolerate.

3. From Instinct to Identity: The Rise of the Narrative Self

One of the most significant shifts in human evolution was the emergence of identity. Early humans lived primarily through instinctual awareness—guided by sensory input, threat detection, and survival drives. Over time, awareness became self-referential. Humans began creating symbolic worlds: language, myth, ritual, religion, culture, and story. Out of this arose the narrative self—the internal storyline that creates continuity across time.

Identity became a meaning-making structure, a social navigation tool, and a container for memory and projection. It made large-scale cooperation possible. It gave shape to values, roles, and shared worlds.

And yet identity also became limitation. Humans began living inside inherited narratives rather than direct experience. The narrative self gave rise to ego—a protective structure that often confuses survival strategies with selfhood. Ego is not an enemy; it is an adaptation. But when it becomes unquestioned center, consciousness stalls inside defense.

The evolution toward synergy requires a new relationship with identity: conscious rather than captive. It asks us to hold identity as a tool—real, influential, and workable —without allowing it to become a prison.

4. Trauma, Fragmentation, and the Disruption of Evolution

No exploration of human evolution is complete without trauma—both individual and

FRAGMENTATION VS. SYNERGY

Comparative States Model

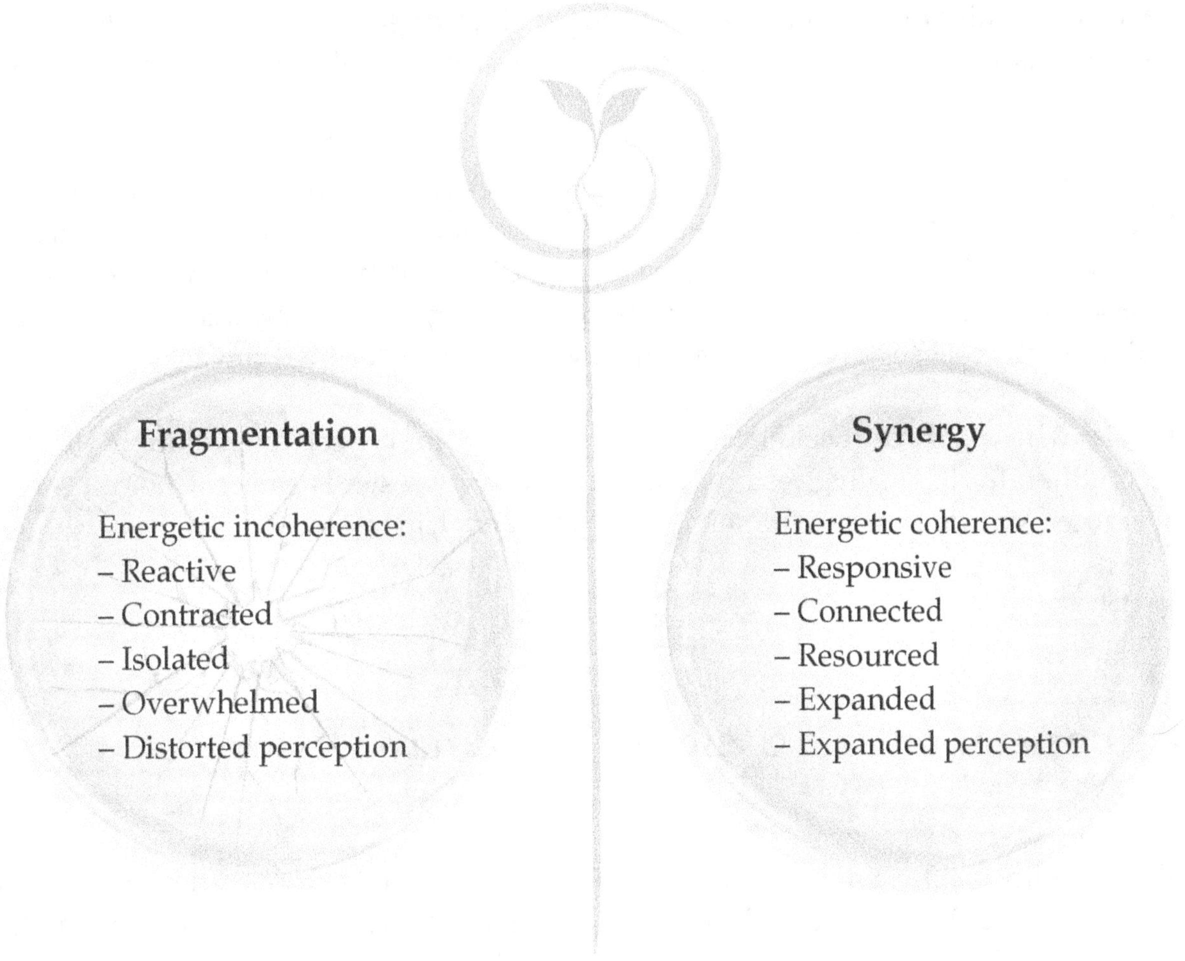

Fragmentation

Energetic incoherence:
- Reactive
- Contracted
- Isolated
- Overwhelmed
- Distorted perception

Synergy

Energetic coherence:
- Responsive
- Connected
- Resourced
- Expanded
- Expanded perception

Figure V.3-A — Human consciousness oscillates between fragmentation and synergy. Fragmentation narrows perception and constricts energy. Synergy expands awareness, restores coherence, and reconnects us to the field. Every moment invites a shift from survival patterns to conscious alignment.

collective. Trauma interrupts development. It constricts awareness, distorts perception, and fragments coherence. And trauma is not only personal. It is cultural, historical, intergenerational, and structural.

War, colonization, religious domination, patriarchy, racism, poverty, exploitation, and coercive systems have shaped human consciousness as profoundly as biology. These forces did not merely harm bodies; they trained nervous systems into vigilance. They installed narratives of separation. They encoded distrust into relational fields. They produced adaptations that made survival possible while limiting higher-order coherence.

Many of humanity's so-called "failures" are not failures of morality or intelligence. They are failures of attunement, safety, and relational coherence. When development is interrupted, individuals and societies become uneven—advanced in some domains and regressed in others. A species cannot stabilize at higher states of awareness while large portions of the collective nervous system remain organized around threat.

This is why personal healing is not separate from collective evolution. It is a precondition for it. Healing restores capacity. Capacity restores choice. Choice restores coherence. And coherence is the soil in which synergy can take root.

5. Cooperation and Synergy in Human History

While conflict is often emphasized in evolutionary narratives, cooperation may be the deeper engine of human survival. Anthropological insight and lived history point to the same underlying principle: humans endured not because they were the strongest, but because they were cooperative, communicative, socially attuned, and capable of shared intention.

Synergy is not new. It is ancient. Communities survived through it, rebuilt through it, and created meaning through it. Humans have always possessed the capacity to generate more together than could be generated alone.

What is new is the call to recognize synergy consciously—not only as a survival adaptation, but as an evolutionary principle. The modern era presses humanity toward intentional synergy: not occasional, not tribal-exclusive, not dependent on a shared enemy, but rooted in coherence, truth, compassion, and sovereignty.

The next step is not simply "more cooperation." It is mature cooperation—cooperation that does not require domination, scapegoating, or the sacrifice of truth.

6. Complexity, Overload, and the Modern Threshold

Humanity now faces an evolutionary pressure unlike any before: hypercomplexity. Historically, humans evolved within systems they could perceive and directly understand. Today we inhabit technological, economic, political, and digital systems that exceed individual comprehension. The result is overwhelm, polarization, information fatigue, relational disconnection, and a strange form of existential displacement—the sensation of living inside forces too large to hold.

The nervous system was not designed for constant global input, perpetual emotional contagion, and nonstop meaning warfare. Without a new mode of awareness, humans oscillate between collapse and rage, dissociation and reactivity, numbness and fanatic certainty. What looks like cultural dysfunction is often nervous-system overload scaled to a species level.

In a hypercomplex environment, survival-based consciousness becomes maladaptive. Synergy becomes an evolutionary adaptation: a perceptual upgrade, a relational upgrade, an energetic upgrade, and a moral upgrade. Evolution is not asking humanity to become harder. It is asking humanity to become more coherent.

7. The Noospheric Turn: Consciousness as a Collective Field

Teilhard de Chardin and later consciousness theorists proposed that humanity is moving toward a noosphere—a field of thought, awareness, and shared meaning encircling the planet. In contemporary terms, this is the recognition that the species is becoming increasingly networked: socially, technologically, emotionally, and energetically.

Developments in network science, social coherence research, group dynamics, and collective-field theories point toward a similar direction: humanity is becoming more interconnected, more interdependent, and more sensitive to global impact. With that interconnection comes a new possibility: collective consciousness as developmental capacity.

This is not hive mind. It is not conformity. It is synergy—sovereign individuals generating higher-order coherence through truth, compassion, and mature relational intelligence. Whenever humans converge in coherent intention, something larger becomes possible.

Synergy is not only personal. It is collective.

8. Evolutionary Tension and the Crisis of Meaning

Every evolutionary leap is preceded by crisis. Humanity is currently facing ecological strain, political fragmentation, psychological overload, relational breakdown, spiritual confusion, and a crisis of truth. Yet beneath these fractures lies an even deeper rupture: a crisis of meaning.

When traditional sources of identity lose coherence—religion, nation, culture, family, stable community—individuals can experience existential vertigo. Some cling to rigid ideology. Some collapse into numbness. Some become addicted to outrage because outrage creates temporary certainty. Often, this is not "irrationality" so much as a nervous system attempting to orient in a world where old maps no longer work.

This crisis is not only collapse. It is transition. Old structures are dissolving; new structures are not yet formed. Synergy is an emergent structure capable of holding this liminal space without resorting to domination, denial, or despair. It offers a form of meaning that does not require illusion: meaning rooted in coherence, interconnection, and embodied participation in collective evolution.

9. The Evolution Toward Synergy: A Developmental Model

Human evolution can be understood as a movement through broad phases of consciousness. Early phases tend to be threat-based and reactive. Later phases become rule-based and belonging-oriented. Then self-reflective consciousness emerges—introspective, questioning, individuating, able to see patterns. Beyond that, synergistic consciousness becomes possible: coherent, compassionate, intuitive, integrative, and purpose-aligned.

These are not rigid categories. They are gradients of capacity. A synergistic human stabilizes in compassion without collapsing discernment. They perceive systems rather than only events. They feel interconnection without losing sovereignty. They embody integrity without moral superiority. They collaborate without self-abandonment. They contribute without domination.

This is the Developer role in the Conscious Role Map: a way of being capable of holding complexity without fragmentation. Synergy is not idealistic. It is adaptive. It offers emotional resilience, perceptual clarity, relational capacity, energetic stability, and creative intelligence. In the modern world, these qualities are not luxuries—they are necessary capacities for a species living inside its own complexity.

10. Collective Trauma and the Great Reorganization

Humanity stands at a crossroads. Old systems—economic, political, ecological, technological—are under strain. These systems reflect the consciousness that built them. As consciousness evolves, systems must reorganize.

But collective trauma complicates the transition. It amplifies reactivity, increases polarization, and distorts perception. We see the symptoms everywhere: conflict escalation, ideological extremism, breakdown of relational trust, fragmentation of shared reality, and rising mental health crises.

Yet beneath these symptoms lies evolutionary tension—the discomfort of a species undergoing reorganization.

Fragmentation vs. Synergy

Dual States Model

Purpose of the Diagram

Figure V.3-B — This diagram visually communicates that fragmentation and synergy are not moral states, but energetic states—two distinct configurations of perception, nervous system regulation, and relational coherence.

Fragmentation	VS	Synergy
Reactive		Responsive
Isolated		Connected
Overwhelmed		Resourced
Distorted Perception		Expanded Perception
Energetic Incoherence		Energetic Coherence

Synergy is not merely connection — it is coherent connection. Fragmentation contracts the field, while synergy expands it. Every choice, sensation, and interaction moves us toward one state or the other.

Synergy is not a slogan meant to soothe this discomfort. It is a stabilizing capacity that can guide the transition: compassion without naivety, integrity without domination, relational repair without denial, energetic alignment without bypassing, and developmental maturity without hierarchy.

11. Synergy as the Future of Human Evolution

When individuals become coherent, relationships tend to stabilize. When relationships stabilize, communities become more workable. When communities become coherent, systems begin to reorganize around new principles.

Synergy is psychologically mature, relationally intelligent, energetically coherent, spiritually grounded, socially adaptive, and ecologically attuned. It is not utopian. It is a developmental milestone.

Humanity's arc bends toward synergy not because it is "nice," but because it is necessary. Survival consciousness can no longer sustain the complexity of the world we have created.

Only synergy can.

Closing Reflection

Humanity is not merely evolving biologically. It is evolving in awareness, compassion, and coherence. The movement from fragmentation to synergy is not only personal—it is historical, collective, and cosmological.

To participate in this evolution, we must understand our place within it: as individuals awakening within a larger field, as cells within a planetary organism, as expressions of consciousness learning to become coherent.

The next movement of this book—Movement II: ALIGN—turns inward to the stabilizing work that makes synergy durable, beginning with the inner terrain where coherence either takes root or collapses.

Evolution is not something happening around us.
It is happening through us.

And synergy is the shape of what comes next.

Synergy in Practice

Choose one area of your life that feels fragmented—internally conflicted, chronically tense, or caught in repeating loops.

Instead of assigning blame to yourself or others, name the competing forces at play (values, needs, fears, roles, survival strategies). Then ask: What is each part trying to protect? What is each part afraid would happen if it softened?

Synergy begins when systems are understood, not condemned.

Orientation Line

This chapter widens the reader's lens from individual awakening to species-level development, showing why coherence is not only personal healing—but evolutionary necessity.

Scholarly Context

The evolutionary framing in this chapter draws from interdisciplinary perspectives across developmental psychology, anthropology, systems theory, trauma studies, and consciousness research. Influential frameworks include stage-based and integrative models of human development (Wilber; Kegan), evolutionary systems and emergence (Corning; Meadows), neuroscience and nervous system regulation in complexity (Siegel; Porges), trauma as developmental disruption at individual and collective scales (van der Kolk; Lanius), cooperative evolution and social attunement (Tomasello), and theories of collective consciousness and noospheric development (Teilhard de Chardin; Laszlo). Together, these perspectives support an understanding of human evolution as not only biological adaptation, but as the progressive expansion of awareness, relational capacity, and coherence at both individual and collective levels.

MOVEMENT II — ALIGN

Where the self becomes a mirror,
and relationship becomes the teacher of coherence.

MOVEMENT II — ALIGN

CHAPTER 4

THE INNER TERRAIN OF SYNERGY

Poetic Insight

Before a forest can thrive, its soil must awaken. And before a human being can embody synergy, the inner world must soften enough for new life to take root. We spend years cultivating the outer layers of ourselves—roles, skills, identities, achievements—while the deeper terrain remains unnamed.

But synergy does not grow in the surface layers. It grows in the quiet underground: where old wounds wait to be witnessed, where emotional weather shapes perception, where ancestral echoes mingle with the present, where the nervous system learns its first language—safety or fear.

This inner terrain is not a battlefield. It is a garden.
And tending it is the beginning of alignment.

Chapter Summary

This chapter transitions the reader from Movement I's conceptual foundations into the lived work of alignment. It explores the inner terrain—the emotional, psychological, somatic, and energetic structures that determine whether synergy becomes accessible or remains disrupted in daily life.

Synergy is not presented as an aspirational mood or moral posture, but as an attuned state that emerges when the internal ecosystem becomes coherent enough to hold awareness, compassion, and relational honesty without fragmentation.

Five core dimensions of inner terrain are examined: Emotional Ecology, Nervous System Regulation, Core Beliefs and Internalized Narratives, Shadow Patterns and Unconscious Drives, and Energetic Integrity. Together, these dimensions establish the conditions under which alignment becomes sustainable—through integration rather than performance, and truth rather than control.

ROLE WINDOW

The Request — Regulating Role

The request arrives, and this time the pause is real. The familiar tightening rises, but it no longer rushes the response. Breath returns before words do. The body is not overridden.

They notice the urge to agree and stay with it. Sensation moves through the chest, the jaw, the hands—information instead of instruction. The moment stretches just enough to be inhabited.

They ask a clarifying question. It is simple, unremarkable, and entirely new. No justification follows. No apology precedes it. The room does not collapse.

The answer comes. With it, relief—and a clearer sense of impact. They feel the edge of what they can hold without losing themselves. For the first time, the boundary is not a wall or a performance. It is a signal.

They respond with more accuracy than before. Not perfectly. But consciously. The system adjusts, subtly. The body remains present.

1. The Terrain Within: Why Inner Alignment Matters

Human beings often attempt transformation through effort—trying to think differently, behave differently, or "become better." But effort alone cannot override the deeper systems that govern perception. The inner terrain is the silent architect of experience: it shapes the meaning we assign, the emotions that arise, and the behaviors we repeat.

Alignment is not simply choosing better outcomes. It is recognizing what is already choosing beneath conscious intention.

This terrain determines what we notice and how we interpret it, what we fear and what we allow, how we attach and what we avoid, how we love, and how we respond to truth. These are not fixed personality traits. They are downstream expressions of nervous system conditioning, emotional patterning, internalized narratives, and unresolved experience.

When the terrain is fragmented, the self fragments.
When the terrain becomes coherent, synergy becomes possible.
(See Figure V.5)

Inner alignment is not about perfection. It is about integration—the capacity to hold complexity without splitting into defense, collapse, or performance.

Vignette — When the Inner Terrain Reveals Itself

It begins as a quiet internal tug.

Two impulses rise at once—one toward speaking, the other toward withdrawing. Neither feels entirely safe. The body holds both simultaneously, calculating—almost unconsciously—which will cost less.

The jaw tightens. The shoulders lift by a fraction. There is pressure behind the eyes, a subtle urgency to resolve something now—even though nothing outside is demanding it.

Emotion moves without language—more sensation than story. A readiness to protect. A readiness to disappear.

Awareness stays.

No side is chosen. No meaning is forced. The tension is allowed to exist without being managed.

After a few breaths, something shifts—not dramatically, not completely. The intensity loosens. The system realizes it does not need to decide yet.

Space appears where urgency had been insisting on control.

Nothing is fixed. Nothing is resolved.
But the self remains whole.

This is integration in motion—not the absence of conflict, but the ability to stay present without fragmenting around it.

Before examining emotions, beliefs, and energy, it helps to name the two primary states the human system cycles between: coherence and fragmentation. Much of what we call growth is simply the gradual reorganization of inner terrain toward coherence—so awareness can remain present even when older protective architectures activate. (See Figure V.4)

Alignment begins the moment the inner world becomes knowable.

2. Emotional Ecology: The Climate of the Inner World

Emotions are not obstacles to clarity; they are signals—often the first evidence that something within the terrain requires attention. Within the emotional ecology of the self, emotions function as movements of energy that shape perception and readiness.

Fear constricts attention.
Anger mobilizes protection.
Sadness softens defenses.
Joy expands capacity.
Shame collapses coherence.
Love integrates disparate states.

Affective neuroscience and somatic psychology affirm a simple truth: emotions shape perception, memory, and meaning-making. When emotions move through awareness, the ecosystem remains balanced. When they stagnate, perception narrows and relational access diminishes.

Synergy requires emotional coherence—the capacity to feel without flooding or dissociation.

Emotional ecology is not secondary to alignment.
It is the soil.

3. Nervous System Regulation: The Gatekeeper of Synergy

If emotions form the climate of the inner terrain, the nervous system provides its structural foundation.

A dysregulated system cannot sustain synergy—not because of weakness, but because synergy requires safety, presence, tolerance for discomfort, and openness to complexity.

Regulation is not the absence of stress.
It is the restoration of response-ability.

Insight may open the door.
Regulation allows the system to walk through it.

4. Core Beliefs and Internalized Narratives

Every individual carries an internal architecture of beliefs shaped by attachment, culture, trauma, and social learning. Many are quiet assumptions that become structural:

I am not enough.
I must stay small.
Love is conditional.
My needs are dangerous.

These beliefs were not freely chosen. They were adaptive.

When left unexamined, adaptation hardens into identity. Narratives become perceptual filters rather than tools.

Alignment deepens when stories are seen as stories—functional once, limiting now.

5. Shadow Patterns and the Unconscious Self

Shadow consists of experience that could not be integrated when it formed. It often appears as defensiveness, projection, people-pleasing, withdrawal, superiority, collapse, or addiction to intensity.

Shadow is not the enemy of alignment.
Shadow is coherence that once felt impossible.

What remains unconscious governs indirectly.
What is brought into awareness loses compulsive power.

Integration restores choice.

6. Energetic Integrity: The Biofield as Inner Terrain

Beyond psychology lies energetic organization. The biofield reflects emotional patterning, belief architecture, trauma history, and truth-tolerance.

Energetic integrity is not protection from others.
It is protection from internal fragmentation.

As coherence increases, intuition clarifies, emotional stability improves, and relational honesty becomes more accessible.

The field stabilizes when the self stops negotiating with its own reality.

7. Inner Honesty: The Transformational Threshold

Inner honesty is perceptual clarity—the willingness to see without distortion.

Without honesty, growth becomes performance.
With honesty, growth becomes reorganization.

When the self stops bargaining with truth, coherence strengthens.

8. Inner Alignment as the Root of Synergy

Inner alignment occurs when emotional coherence, regulation, narrative clarity, shadow integration, energetic integrity, and compassion begin to harmonize.

Synergy is not achieved through effort.
It is cultivated through coherence.

Closing Reflection

The inner terrain carries both distortion and wisdom, protection and genuine knowing. Synergy honors all of it—while granting authority to none.

As coherence deepens, the soul does not erupt; it emerges—quietly, steadily—like light finding its way through stone.

Movement II continues with integrity: the force that transforms inner alignment into embodied presence.

Synergy in Practice

Begin with a gentle body scan. Notice where the system is braced or withdrawn.
Ask: Is this tension—or protection?

Invite a five-percent softening, if possible.
Then ask: What is one honest sentence my body is holding right now?

Write it down.
Permission precedes regulation.

Orientation Line

This chapter stabilizes the inner ecosystem so synergy can arise from regulation rather than force.

Scholarly Context

This chapter draws from trauma-informed psychology, somatic and affective neuroscience, attachment theory, narrative psychology, depth psychology, and emerging biofield research. Contemporary trauma science emphasizes that emotional states and nervous system regulation fundamentally shape perception, behavior, and relational capacity (Porges; van der Kolk; Siegel). Attachment research demonstrates how early relational environments shape core beliefs and emotional patterning (Bowlby; Ainsworth). Depth psychology and trauma-informed models view shadow and defensive patterns as adaptive strategies rather than pathologies (Jung; Siegel). Biofield and psychophysiological coherence research suggests measurable correlations between emotional regulation, belief coherence, and energetic stability (Oschman; McCraty). Together, these perspectives support the chapter's central premise: synergy arises not through effortful self-control, but through integrated coherence across emotional, somatic, cognitive, and energetic systems.

MOVEMENT II — ALIGN

CHAPTER 5

THE ENERGETICS OF PERCEPTION

Poetic Insight

The world is not given to us as it is.

It arrives filtered through the currents of our nervous system,

colored by memory, shaped by emotion, and refracted through the

subtle frequencies that ripple through the field of our awareness.

Two people can stand in the same moment and live in different

worlds—not because truth is subjective, but because perception is

energetic: an ongoing interplay between the inner field of the

perceiver and the outer landscape they are attempting to meet.

To understand perception is to understand how consciousness

translates vibration into meaning—how energy becomes story, and

how synergy becomes possible only when perception itself

becomes clear.

Chapter Summary

This chapter explores perception not as a passive reception of information, but as an energetic event—one that emerges from the continuous interaction between the human biofield, the nervous system, emotional memory, relational context, and cognitive interpretation. Building on the inner terrain established in Chapter 4, we examine how internal coherence or fragmentation shapes the meaning we assign to experience, often without awareness.

Perception is shown to be a whole-system process involving body, field, and mind simultaneously. Trauma, regulation, resonance, intuition, and development are not secondary influences on perception; they are constitutive of it. Because synergy depends on accurate perception—of self, other, and situation—learning how perception forms, distorts, and clarifies becomes essential to alignment.

Perception is not merely cognitive.

It is relational, somatic, energetic, and developmental.

1. Perception as an Energetic Process

Perception begins long before thought.

Every moment generates a cascade of signals that move through the body faster than conscious awareness can track. Some signals are sensory—sound, light, temperature. Others are relational and emotional, carried through tone, posture, timing, and presence. Still others register beneath conscious detection entirely, arriving as subtle impressions, intuitive impulses, or quiet shifts in the field sensed by the body before the mind has language.

These signals are registered first in the biofield and nervous system. The brain does not initiate perception; it organizes perception after the fact. Meaning is constructed downstream from sensation. In this sense, perception is energetic first and cognitive second.

Most perception is automated. Energy is registered, the nervous system shifts, emotion forms, cognition assigns interpretation, behavior follows, and outcomes reinforce the original pattern.

Synergy becomes possible when awareness enters this sequence earlier—before narrative hardens, before reaction takes over, before defense defines meaning.

BIOFIELD
Pre-cognitive sensing
Intervention here alters the entire sequence.
NERVOUS SYSTEM
Signal translation
Perception as an
Energetic Cascade
EMOTION
COGNITION
INTERPRETATION
Narrative meaning

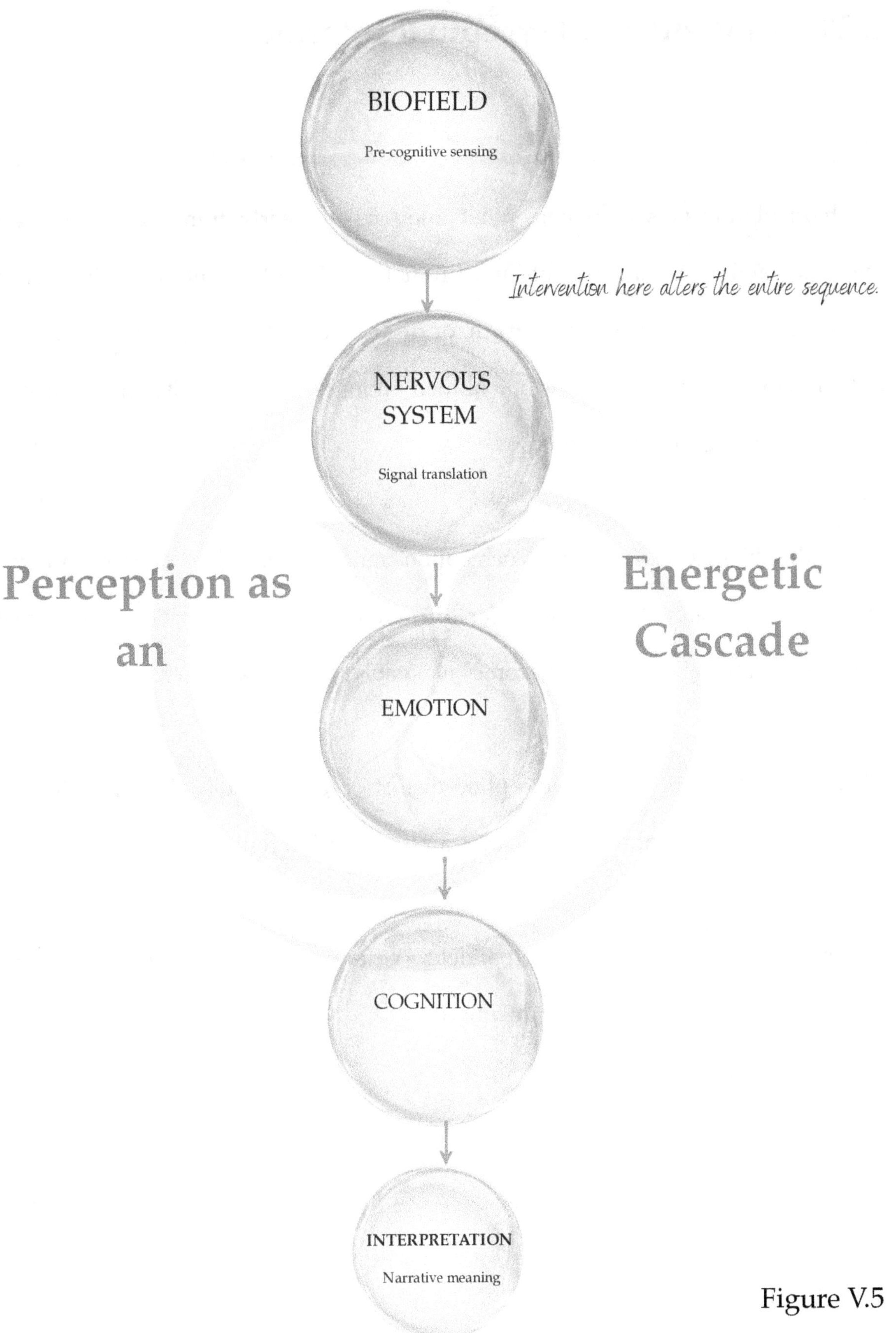

Figure V.5

2. The Biofield as a Perceptual Interface

The biofield functions as a perceptual interface—an early translator of relational, emotional, and environmental information that the mind later interprets. This is why people often sense danger, safety, truth, or dissonance before they can explain it. The system registers unspoken tension, hidden motives, compatibility, and instability without requiring conscious analysis.

When the biofield is coherent, perception tends to become clearer and more trustworthy. Emotional signal is easier to regulate. Intuition functions with greater accuracy. Relational complexity becomes navigable rather than overwhelming.

When the field is fragmented, perception distorts. Signal-to-noise decreases. Intuition becomes unreliable. Emotional static increases. Confusion replaces clarity.

Synergy requires a coherent perceptual field. Without coherence, perception cannot be trusted—regardless of intellect or intention.

3. The Nervous System as Energetic Translator

Everything we perceive is filtered through the state of the nervous system. A regulated system reads the same information very differently than a dysregulated one.

When regulation is present, ambiguity can be met with curiosity rather than threat. Relational cues are read more accurately. Emotional nuance becomes tolerable. Compassion becomes physiologically accessible.

When the system is dysregulated—whether in sympathetic activation or dorsal collapse—perception narrows. Neutral cues are misread as hostile. Silence may feel rejecting. Boundaries may feel aggressive. Guidance may feel controlling. Access to higher-order awareness diminishes, and intuitive signal becomes distorted or inaccessible.

This is why somatic and emotional healing are not optional add-ons to conscious work. They are prerequisites for perceptual accuracy. Without regulation, synergy is not merely difficult; it is structurally unstable.

4. Trauma and the Distortion of Perception

Trauma alters perception at every level: energetic, emotional, somatic, cognitive, and relational. A traumatized system does not perceive what is; it perceives what was.

Residual imprints shape interpretation in the present moment. A safe gesture may feel threatening. A neutral silence may feel rejecting. A loving presence may feel overwhelming. A boundary may feel like abandonment. These responses are not failures of character; they are perceptual echoes.

Trauma creates energetic ghosts—unresolved patterns that haunt the present by masquerading as current reality. Without awareness, the loop reinforces itself: the field registers signal, the nervous system activates old protection, the mind assigns meaning based on memory, the body responds defensively, and the outcome is encoded as confirmation.

Healing interrupts this loop by restoring temporal accuracy—updating the system's understanding of what is happening now.

5. Resonance and Dissonance: The Energetics of Connection

Perception is inherently relational. We do not only perceive the world; we perceive one another.

Resonance occurs when two fields are compatible or coherent. It is often felt as ease rather than intensity—a quiet openness that does not require effort, a sense of trust that arises without persuasion.

Dissonance often announces itself through contraction: pressure in the body, irritation without clear cause, confusion that resists resolution, or a heaviness that makes engagement feel effortful. Attention fragments. Emotional noise increases. Boundaries tighten.

Resonance is not agreement, and dissonance is not judgment. Both are informational signals arising from field interaction.

Synergy requires the capacity to sense resonance without merging, recognize dissonance without rejecting, and remain regulated in both—so discernment can stay compassionate, and compassion can remain discerning.

6. The Heart–Brain System and Coherence

The heart is not merely a mechanical pump. It functions as a regulator of emotional and energetic states and generates a rhythmic electromagnetic field that extends beyond the body and interfaces with the environment.

When the heart is coherent, perception stabilizes. Reactivity decreases. Cognitive clarity improves. Intuition becomes more reliable. Relational presence deepens. The system moves from fragmentation toward harmony.

The heart acts as a bridge between energy and meaning. The mind interprets, but the heart orients. When these systems align, both inner and outer worlds become more navigable without distortion.

Synergy depends on this coherence—not as an idea, but as a lived physiological and energetic reality.

7. Cognitive Filters and Energetic Bias

Perception is shaped not only by energy and emotion but also by cognitive filters formed through experience—trauma-based expectations, relational templates, cultural narratives, identity constructs, moral frameworks, spiritual interpretations, and habitual mental patterns.

Energetic bias arises when unresolved internal states shape the meaning assigned to external signal. A person afraid of abandonment may interpret neutrality as rejection. A person afraid of conflict may interpret boundaries as aggression. A person wounded by authority may experience guidance as control.

These biases are rarely intentional. They operate automatically, shaping perception beneath conscious choice. Synergy requires the gradual cultivation of less biased perception—one grounded in internal clarity rather than emotional residue.

A Lived Moment of Discernment

A choice presents itself quietly. There is no obvious right answer—only competing values pressing for attention. Each option carries consequence. Each stirs a different sensation in the body.

One path feels cleaner but tighter. The other feels uncertain but open. The nervous system leans, then hesitates. Habit searches for a rule to follow.

Awareness pauses the impulse to decide quickly. Sensation is tracked without justification. The subtle signals beneath preference are noticed—the contraction that seeks certainty, the openness that tolerates ambiguity.

Nothing is resolved immediately. Integrity is not performed. The system remains with what is true rather than what is comfortable. In that stillness, clarity begins to form—not as certainty, but as alignment.

This is discernment embodied—not choosing perfectly, but choosing from coherence rather than fear.

8. Intuition as an Energetic Mind

Intuition is not mystical. It is an integrated perceptual system—combining subtle energy, bodily sensation, emotional signal, unconscious processing, relational cues, and pattern recognition.

When the inner terrain is coherent and the nervous system regulated, intuition tends to function with greater accuracy. When fear, anxiety, unresolved trauma, or hypervigilance dominate perception, intuitive signal becomes distorted—often louder, more urgent, and less stable.

The difference is not intensity.
It is quality.

Synergy depends not on intuitive drama, but on intuitive clarity.

9. Perception Across the Developmental Arc

As individuals evolve through the Conscious Role Map—Character, Player, Developer—perception expands in depth and dimensionality.

In the Character role, perception is survival-oriented and filtered through inherited narratives and defensive patterning.

In the Player role, perception becomes more curious, reflective, and increasingly capable of pattern recognition.

In the Developer role, perception becomes more coherent, systemic, compassionate, and energetically attuned—capable of holding nuance without collapse.

Perception evolves as consciousness evolves. Synergy emerges when perception becomes multidimensional and stable enough to remain accurate under pressure.

10. Interpretation as an Energetic Act

Even after perception occurs, interpretation remains an energetic act. Two people can perceive the same event and assign entirely different meanings based on emotional state, nervous system regulation, belief structures, energetic imprint, and trauma history.

Interpretation is where synergy is either amplified or lost.

Synergistic interpretation is regulated, truthful, spacious, and compassionate. It allows complexity without collapse and difference without threat.

Micro-Practice: Breath Before Interpretation

The next time something stirs you—a message, a tone of voice, a glance—pause for a single breath before assigning meaning. Feel the sensation in the chest or abdomen without rushing toward explanation.

Ask quietly: What is my body registering before my mind decides what it means?

Let this breath widen the space between sensation and story. Clarity enters through the opening created when reaction subsides.

Closing Reflection

Perception is not a window.

It is a mirror—reflecting not only the world, but the state of the one who is perceiving.

To cultivate synergy, we must soften the internal architecture that distorts perception and refine the energetic clarity through which meaning forms. When perception becomes coherent, life becomes more intelligible. Relationships become more navigable. Truth becomes more bearable. Awareness becomes liberating.

Chapter 6 turns toward integrity—the harmonic structure that stabilizes perception and aligns the self with truth.

Synergy in Practice

Choose one recurring reaction you've had recently—irritation, defensiveness, shutdown, urgency, or doubt. Write down the activating moment in one sentence. Then write the meaning your system immediately assigned.

Ask gently:

- Is this meaning current—or conditioned?

- Is this interpretation arising from clarity—or from protection?

- What becomes possible if I pause before I conclude?

Do not replace the meaning. Simply create space around it. Let awareness loosen

the grip of certainty.

Orientation Line

This chapter refines perception at the level of field, body, and interpretation so integrity can emerge from clarity rather than reactivity.

Scholarly Context

The model of perception presented in this chapter draws from interdisciplinary research across neuroscience, psychophysiology, trauma studies, biofield science, and consciousness research. Foundational influences include embodied perception and emotion–cognition coupling (Damasio), interpersonal neurobiology and state-dependent perception (Siegel), trauma-induced perceptual distortion and temporal misalignment (van der Kolk; Lanius), nervous system regulation and autonomic filtering (Porges), heart–brain coherence and psychophysiological synchronization (McCraty), biofield-mediated perception and subtle signal processing (Oschman; Jain & Mills), and developmental models of perception and meaning-making (Kegan). Together, these perspectives support an understanding of perception as a whole-system, energetic, and relational process rather than a purely cognitive function.

MOVEMENT II — ALIGN

CHAPTER 6

THE HARMONICS OF INTEGRITY

Poetic Insight

Integrity is not a rule.
It is a resonance.

It is the quiet vibration that arises when who we are, what we feel,
what we believe, and how we act fall into alignment.

Integrity is the frequency of truth within us—a tuning fork that
rings clean when we stand in coherence and dulls when we
fracture ourselves for safety, belonging, or illusion.

This chapter is not about correctness. It is about wholeness—about
the subtle harmonics that emerge when the self is no longer split
between inner knowing and outward behavior.

Synergy begins when the inner and outer worlds speak the same
language.

Chapter Summary

Integrity is often misunderstood as moral purity or ethical behavior. In the context of Conscious Synergy, integrity refers to coherence—the alignment of internal states, actions, values, energy, and truth. It is not simply something we do. It is something we become as the inner terrain stabilizes and the self stops fragmenting under pressure.

This chapter explores integrity as a biological and energetic necessity, a psychological stabilizer, a relational anchor, a spiritual practice, and a developmental achievement. We examine how fragmentation disrupts integrity, how trauma divides the self into adaptive parts, and how reclaiming integrity restores coherence. We explore the relationship between integrity and frequency, drawing on Hawkins' levels of consciousness, somatic regulation, and energetic alignment.

Finally, we introduce the Harmonic Model of Integrity, showing how layers of the self converge to create the resonance required for synergy. Integrity becomes the inner chord that allows truth to move through the whole system without distortion.

ROLE WINDOW

The Request — Integrated Role

The request arrives, and the body registers it without alarm. Sensation is present, but steady. There is no urgency to answer, no need to disappear. The pause feels natural now.

They listen fully—to the request, and to themselves. Capacity is clear. Values are online. What can be offered and what cannot are no longer blurred by fear or obligation.

They respond with honesty rather than reflex. The words are simple. The boundary is named without defense and without explanation. It does not require permission to exist.

There is a brief moment of tension—then something settles. The choice aligns. Relief is quiet, but unmistakable. Integrity is not something they perform. It is something they feel.

The system adjusts. They remain intact.

1. Integrity as Coherence, Not Morality

Integrity is the state in which the inner world and the outer life are no longer in contradiction. It is the convergence of thought, emotion, action, boundaries, values, nervous system signal, energetic field, and inner truth into a single coherent pattern. When integrity is present, a person may still be imperfect, still learning, still tender—but they are no longer split. The system speaks with one voice.

This reframes integrity from a moralized concept to a structural state of being. A person can behave "correctly" while out of integrity—performing goodness while concealing inner incongruence. A person can also violate social expectation while remaining deeply aligned with truth. Integrity is not compliance. It is congruence. It is wholeness.

Fragmentation is not always dramatic. Often it looks like quiet self-betrayal, subtle silencing, or emotional editing performed so consistently that the self can no longer feel what it knows.

Vignette — The Smallest Fracture

A simple question lands: Are you okay?

The mouth answers before the body does. "I'm fine." It comes out smooth, practiced—almost automatic.

But the chest doesn't agree. Something in the ribs tightens, like a hand closing around a thread. The throat thickens slightly. The breath stays high.

There is no crisis. No obvious reason to correct anything. Just a familiar internal split: what is offered outward, and what is quietly held back.

Awareness catches it midstream.

Not as blame. Not as performance. As sensation—a subtle static in the field. The body registers the cost of the phrase I'm fine the way it registers a small lie: a faint contraction, a dimming of signal.

Nothing is confessed. Nothing is explained.

A pause opens.

And in that pause, the next sentence becomes possible—small enough to feel safe, true enough to restore coherence.

2. The Science of Integrity: Coherence Across Systems

Integrity is not only philosophical. Coherence is a whole-system phenomenon—reflected in the body, the brain, and the field.

When the nervous system is coherent, perception stabilizes and the inner witness remains accessible. When the system is incoherent, interpretation distorts, reactivity increases, and decision-making becomes fear-driven—even when the person believes they are being rational.

Neurobiologically, integrity is supported by regulation. In a regulated state, the prefrontal cortex can hold nuance. Emotional centers integrate rather than hijack behavior. Relational presence improves because the system is not defending against imagined threat. Ethical reasoning strengthens because the mind can hold complexity instead of collapsing into survival binaries.

Psychologically, integrity appears when actions reflect values and narratives align with truth. Emotions inform rather than overwhelm. Shame loosens its grip on identity. Shadow becomes visible instead of governing from below.

Energetically, integrity appears as coherence in the biofield. Intuition clarifies. Boundaries stabilize. Resonance becomes easier to sense. Dissonance becomes easier to name.

Integrity is multidimensional convergence: biology, psyche, and field aligning into stable inner truth.

3. Integrity and Truth: The Energetic Relationship

Integrity and truth are inseparable. Truth is not only factual—it is energetic accuracy: alignment between what is happening, what we feel, what we say, and what we choose.

When truth is avoided, the system tightens. Static increases. The field becomes noisier. We fall out of integrity in ways that are often socially rewarded: betraying our knowing, suppressing emotion, performing for approval, agreeing to avoid conflict, staying silent to preserve belonging, hiding parts of ourselves to feel safe.

Each fracture seems small. But fractures accumulate. They distort perception, weaken trust, and collapse frequency—not as punishment, but as consequence.

Synergy requires truth-tolerance: the capacity to remain present with what is real without weaponizing it and without fleeing from it. Integrity is what makes truth survivable inside the system.

4. Trauma and the Fragmentation of Integrity

Trauma fractures integrity structurally, not morally. A traumatized system often learns to disconnect from feeling, minimize needs, hyper-adapt to others, suppress intuition, override boundaries, and mistake collapse for peace. These strategies are intelligent. They preserved survival when truth was unsafe.

But survival strategies divide the self into parts: the part that performs, the part that hides, the part that endures, the part that dissociates, the part that anticipates threat. Truth becomes dangerous. Authenticity becomes risky. Synergy cannot take root in divided soil.

Restoring integrity means reclaiming what splintered under pressure and bringing it back into coherent internal relationship—so truth no longer threatens survival.

5. Emotional Integrity: Feeling Without Fragmenting

Emotional integrity means feeling fully without being ruled by feeling, and without abandoning feeling to please others. This requires the nervous system to remain present while emotional energy moves.

Fragmentation often cycles through suppression and explosion, dissociation and performance, numbness and projection. Emotional integrity does not mean "good emotions." It means truth moving through the emotional body without distortion.

As this capacity strengthens, reactivity decreases. Transparency increases. The system becomes capable of sustaining synergy under pressure—not because emotion disappears, but because it becomes integrated signal instead of destabilizing force.

6. Cognitive Integrity: Clear Thinking as a Result of Coherence

Cognitive integrity is the ability to think without self-deception—without ego-protection, shame-avoidance, trauma bias, projection, superiority, or bypassing. It is not brilliance. It is honesty.

Cognitive integrity arises when regulation and emotional coherence are present. In that state, the mind can ask a simple, radical question:

What is true right now, without distortion?

Without cognitive integrity, perception becomes unreliable. With it, interpretation becomes more spacious, nuanced, and less reactive—essential conditions for synergy.

7. Energetic Integrity: When the Field Becomes Clean

Energetic integrity is the vibrational alignment between the inner and outer self. When it is present, the field feels steadier. Intuition strengthens. Boundaries are felt rather than forced. The body stops living in contradiction with truth.

When it is absent, the field often feels noisy or collapsed. Intuition becomes unreliable. Relationships feel confusing. The body carries contradictions the mind has not named.

Energetic integrity is the frequency of honesty—truth not only recognized, but embodied.

8. Relational Integrity: Coherence Between Self and Other

Integrity is relational as well as personal. Relational integrity is meeting another person without manipulation, without self-abandonment, and without coercion. It includes truthful communication, regulated conflict, impact awareness, willingness to repair, and refusal to use emotional distortion as leverage.

Relational integrity is the foundation of trust. It does not guarantee agreement, but it creates a field where truth can be held without weaponization. In that field, relationships become navigable rather than destabilizing.

9. The Harmonic Model of Integrity

Integrity is harmonic—like notes in a chord that must align to create resonance. When one note is dissonant, the chord loses stability. The self contains layers that must converge for integrity to become durable.

THE HARMONICS OF INTEGRITY

Integrity is not a rule — it is resonance.

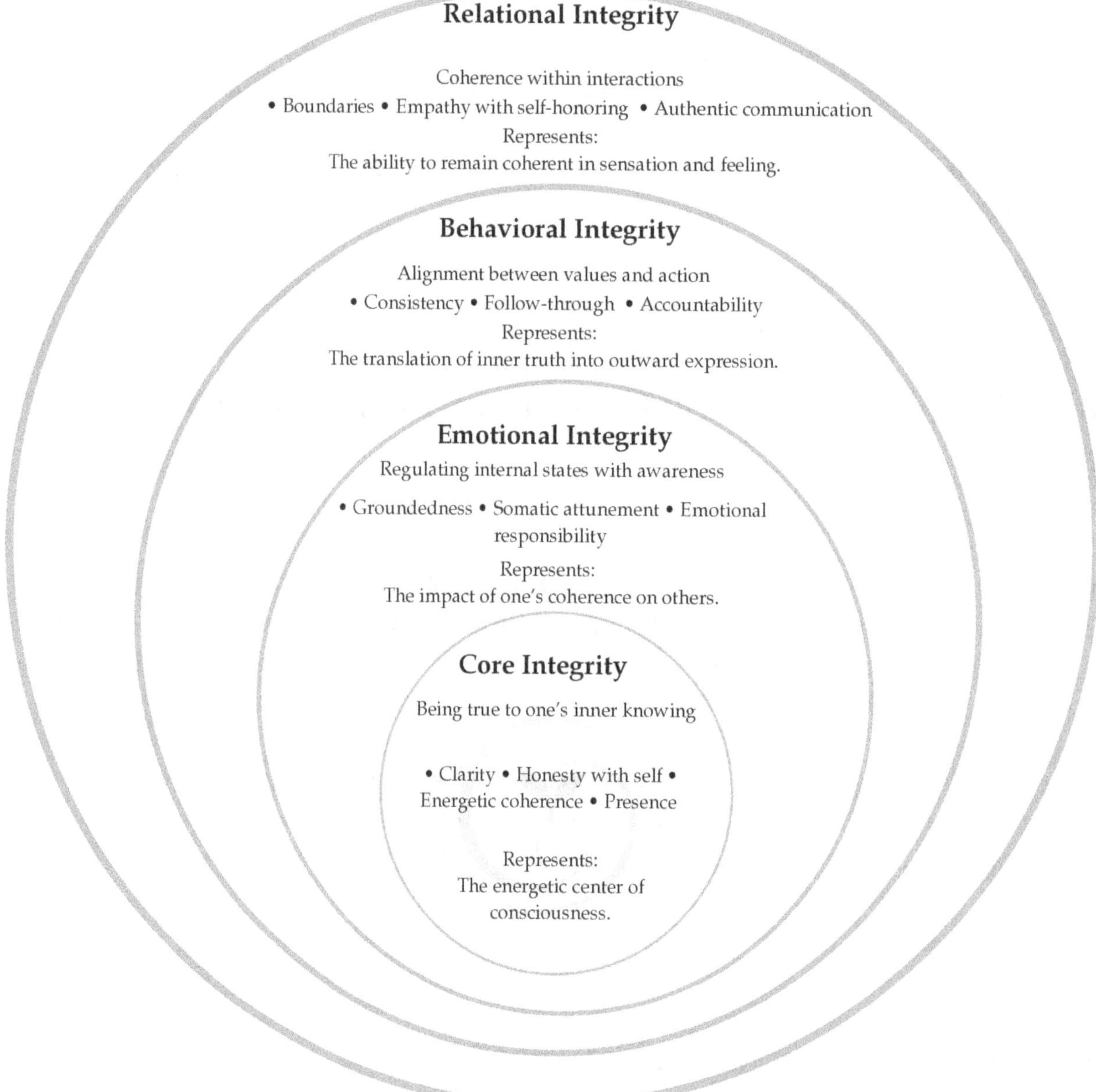

Figure V.6 — When our inner state aligns with our actions and relationships, coherence expands outward like harmonics through the field. Integrity is the foundation of synergy, the architecture that transforms personal alignment into collective evolution.

The Harmonic Model of Integrity includes five layers: somatic integrity, emotional integrity, cognitive integrity, energetic integrity, and relational integrity.

When these layers align, the individual becomes capable of sustaining synergy. Hawkins' insight appears here in another form: truth is higher-frequency because it is more coherent. Integrity makes that coherence livable—not as ideology, but as embodied resonance. (See Figure V.6)

10. Living in Integrity: A Practice of Embodied Synergy

Integrity is not a state achieved once. It is a continuous practice of alignment. It requires reflection, regulation, honesty, discernment, courage, humility, and compassionate return.

Integrity is not perfection. It is presence. It is the willingness to stop splitting the self into acceptable and unacceptable parts—and to meet the whole self with enough truth that coherence can stabilize.

In this way, integrity becomes a spiritual practice: a daily tuning of the instrument of the self.

Micro-Practice: Realignment in a Single Sentence

Once today, name quietly—just to yourself—one place where your actions and your truth feel slightly out of sync. No judgment. Only honesty.

Ask: What is the smallest adjustment that would bring me closer to coherence?

Let the body register the relief that comes with alignment. Integrity deepens through tiny, sincere recalibrations—through the humble return to what is true.

Closing Reflection

Integrity is the harmonic structure of the soul—the resonance that emerges when nothing within us is at war.

It does not demand purity.
It invites coherence.

Synergy cannot exist without integrity.
Integrity cannot exist without truth.
Truth cannot exist without awareness.

In the next chapter, we turn toward compassion—the field through which integrity becomes relational, and through which synergy becomes embodied in connection with others.

Synergy in Practice

Recall one recent moment where your inner truth and outward action were misaligned, even subtly. Name what you did, and name what you knew.

Now recall one moment of quiet congruence—where what you felt, thought, and did were aligned. Notice the difference in your body and field.

Ask gently:

- Where do I most often fracture for safety or belonging?
- What would a five-percent return to truth look like today?
- What boundary, sentence, or small choice would reduce inner static?

Choose one micro-adjustment you can make within the next 24 hours. Keep it small enough that your nervous system can stay regulated while you follow through. Integrity becomes durable through repeated returns, not dramatic declarations.

Orientation Line

This chapter stabilizes coherence across body, mind, field, and relationship so truth can move through the whole system without fracture.

Scholarly Context

The framing of integrity in this chapter draws from interdisciplinary research across neuroscience, psychology, trauma studies, biofield science, ethics, and consciousness research. Key influences include coherence and psychophysiological regulation (Siegel; McCraty), trauma-related self-fragmentation and integration (van der Kolk; Lanius), moral reasoning and identity coherence (Kohlberg; Haidt), shadow integration and unconscious patterning (Jung), and field-based models of consciousness and frequency (Hawkins; Oschman). Together, these perspectives support integrity as a whole-system phenomenon—biological, psychological, relational, and energetic—rather than a purely moral or behavioral construct.

MOVEMENT II — ALIGN

CHAPTER 7

THE FIELD OF COMPASSION

Poetic Insight

Compassion is not sentiment.

It is perception in its purest form—the ability to recognize the self in the other without losing the truth of either.

It is the spaciousness that remains when defensiveness dissolves, when fear loosens its grip, when the heart opens just enough for two worlds to touch.

Compassion is not weakness. It is coherence expressed as relationship—a frequency strong enough to hold pain without absorbing it, to witness truth without collapsing, to extend understanding without self-betrayal.

This is the field in which synergy becomes alive.

Chapter Summary

Compassion is the emotional and energetic foundation of synergy. This chapter reframes compassion beyond sentimental or moral definitions, presenting it as regulated presence, energetic field, and developmental achievement—emerging from the interplay of awareness, integrity, and attunement. Compassion is not a technique performed on demand; it is a coherent state that arises when the system is safe enough to remain open without becoming porous.

We explore the neurobiology of compassion and why safety is a prerequisite for genuine care. We distinguish compassion from empathic overload and relational enmeshment, and examine how trauma shapes one's capacity for compassion—sometimes amplifying it into overextension, sometimes constricting it into numbness. We reframe compassion fatigue as a symptom of incoherence rather than proof that compassion is unsustainable.

Finally, we explore compassion as frequency and collective field influence. When coherent, compassion reorganizes perception, stabilizes relationship, reduces polarization, and becomes a bridge from separation into synergy.

Compassion is not a performance.
It is a field—a resonance that allows coherent connection to emerge.

ROLE WINDOW

The Request — Integrated Role with Compassion

The request arrives, and they receive it fully. There is space to listen without bracing, to sense the need beneath the words without absorbing it as their own. The body remains grounded.

They feel the familiar edge of capacity and honor it. The boundary is clear, but it is not rigid. It moves with discernment, shaped by honesty rather than fear.

They respond with care. The limit is named without sharpness, the offering without obligation. There is room for the other's disappointment, confusion, or relief—none of it needs to be fixed.

The moment holds. Connection remains. No one is diminished.

Compassion here is not self-sacrifice.
It is presence that does not abandon itself.

1. Compassion as a State of Consciousness

Compassion is often described as an emotion, but in the context of Conscious Synergy it functions more accurately as a state of consciousness. It arises when awareness is present, the nervous system is regulated, the heart is coherent, integrity is stable, and truth can be tolerated without defensiveness. In that state, care is not forced. It becomes natural—because the system is no longer preoccupied with protection.

Compassion is not the urge to rescue or fix. It is the capacity to remain open in the presence of suffering—our own or another's—without collapsing into it and without hardening against it. It is the middle space where understanding can exist alongside honesty, where warmth can coexist with clarity.

This is why compassion is developmental. It requires integration across systems: the felt resonance of empathy, the cognitive ability to take perspective, the somatic stability that sustains presence, the boundary awareness that protects coherence, and the honesty to acknowledge reality without distortion. Compassion is not one trait. It is an architecture.

2. The Neurobiology of Compassion: Safety as a Prerequisite

Compassion becomes inaccessible when the nervous system is in a threat state. In dysregulation, defensive patterns dominate, nuance collapses, and the body commits more energy to protection than connection. This is why compassion is not merely a moral choice. Often, it is a regulated state.

Polyvagal theory clarifies the mechanism: the ventral vagal system—associated with connection, presence, and attunement—forms the physiological foundation of compassion. When ventral activation is available, the face softens, the voice steadies, heart rhythm stabilizes, attention widens, and the system can hold emotional reality without perceiving it as threat.

Compassion, then, is the biological expression of safety. It does not require the absence of pain. It requires sufficient regulation to remain open while pain is present.

Vignette — Compassion Without Self-Abandonment

The conversation slows unexpectedly.

Someone shares something painful—unfinished, unpolished, still tender. The words arrive unevenly, carrying more weight than clarity. The body registers it immediately: a pull forward, a tightening in the chest, the familiar impulse to help—soothe—make it better.

Awareness arrives before the impulse completes.

The breath deepens slightly. The feet press into the floor. The urgency to rescue is noticed—not judged, not indulged. Simply recognized as familiar. A learned response, not a command.

Nothing is fixed. Nothing is taken on.

Instead, presence settles.

The body remains open without leaning in too far. The heart stays engaged without spilling over. Boundaries are felt, not enforced. There is room for the other person's pain—and room for the self to remain intact within it.

When words come, they are simple.

They do not promise solutions. They do not minimize. They do not absorb responsibility. They reflect what is heard and leave space for what is still forming.

Something softens—not dramatically, but perceptibly.

The exchange ends without exhaustion. No residue lingers. No self-erasure occurred.

Compassion moved through the moment without requiring sacrifice.

The system remains coherent.

3. Empathy, Compassion, and Enmeshment: Knowing the Difference

Empathy is the capacity to feel another person's emotional state within oneself. This can be a gift—but empathy without regulation can overwhelm. When resonance enters a system that cannot metabolize it, the result is often absorption, boundary collapse,

Compassion as a Regulated Field

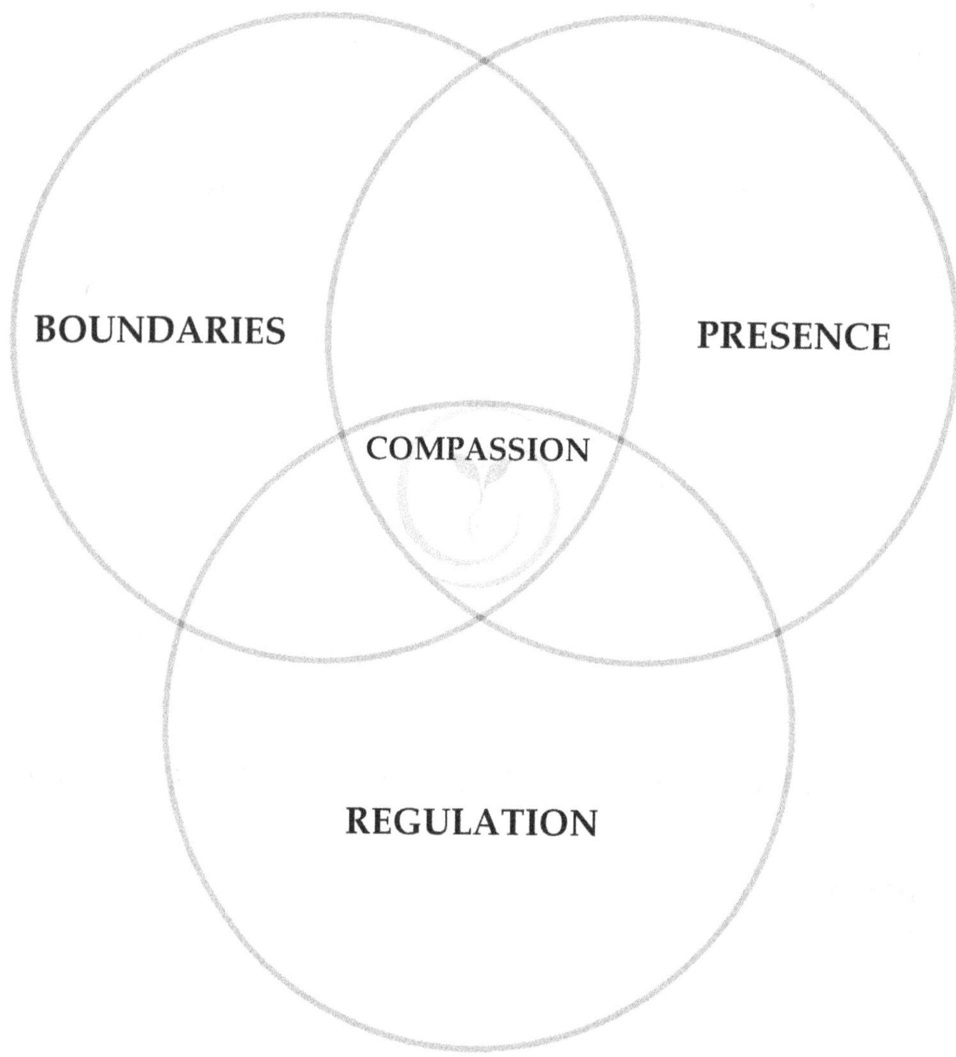

Figure V.7 — Compassion arises not from effort, but from the simultaneous presence of boundaries, regulation, and presence.

resentment, or exhaustion. The body treats another's pain as an emergency inside the self.

Enmeshment goes further: losing oneself in another's emotional experience. It can masquerade as compassion, but is often driven by fear, insecurity, unmet attachment needs, or the learned belief that safety is earned through over-giving. It is not love. It is survival dressed as virtue.

Compassion is different. Compassion holds another's experience with openness, clarity, and regulated presence—without absorbing it, fixing it, or collapsing into it. Compassion is resonance without fusion. It is the middle way between detachment and overwhelm, where care remains real because the self remains intact.

4. Trauma and the Barriers to Compassion

Trauma distorts compassion in two primary directions, and both are protective.

Some develop hyper-compassion—overextension that looks like compulsive rescuing, absorbing others' pain, endless giving, or carrying responsibility that is not theirs.

This pattern often traces back to parentification, guilt conditioning, fear of abandonment, or learned self-erasure. The system equates care with survival.

Others develop hypo-compassion—constriction. Numbness, avoidance, difficulty empathizing, or "I can't feel anything" is often not coldness, but overwhelm. The system learned that feeling was dangerous or unsupported and tightened into protection.

Synergy requires integration of both patterns—not suppression of compassion, but restoration of regulated compassion: the form that can remain open without leaving the self.

5. Compassion as Energetic Frequency: The Field of the Heart

Compassion is not only psychological. It is vibrational.

Heart-coherence research suggests that coherent emotional states such as compassion stabilize internal regulation and influence relational dynamics. Compassion, in this sense, is not merely an inner feeling. It is an organizing frequency. (See Figure V.6)

When compassion is coherent, perception softens without becoming naïve. The nervous system steadies. Defensive ego strategies quiet. Truth becomes easier to tolerate. Presence becomes easier to maintain. And this coherence can influence others —supporting co-regulation, reducing relational threat, and increasing the likelihood that honesty can land without harm.

Compassion is an energetic stabilizer. It signals safety—not as softness without discernment, but as steadiness with heart.

6. Compassion, Boundaries, and Truth

Compassion without boundaries becomes enmeshment. Boundaries without compassion become rigidity. Synergy requires both.

Compassion with boundaries allows us to witness pain without absorbing it, speak truth without aggression, stay connected without merging, and support others without self-abandonment. Boundaries keep compassion honest. They prevent care from becoming self-sacrifice and prevent empathy from becoming fusion.

Truth is not opposed to compassion. Often, truth is the highest form of compassion. Compassion does not hide reality—it carries reality gently, clearly, and without cruelty. Compassion is not "being nice." It is being real with softness.

7. Compassion Fatigue: A Symptom of Incoherence

Compassion fatigue is rarely caused by compassion itself. More often, it arises from fragmentation: over-absorbing, over-functioning, over-carrying—driven by trauma patterns, hyper-empathy, enmeshment, lack of boundaries, chronic dysregulation, self-neglect, suppressed personal truth, or the compulsive performance of strength.

Regulated, coherent, boundaried compassion does not exhaust. It sustains. If "compassion" drains energy, something else is happening—something is being carried that is not meant to be carried, or something within the self is being abandoned in the act of giving.

8. Compassion as Mirror: Seeing the Self in the Other

Compassion is not pity. It is recognition.

It is the ability to see beyond behavior into the conditions that shaped it—to recognize pain beneath defensiveness, shame beneath anger, fear beneath control, loneliness beneath withdrawal. This is not indulgence. It is perceptual clarity.

Trauma shapes behavior. Fear shapes communication. Shame shapes defenses. Compassion sees the architecture behind the expression. It does not excuse harm, but it dissolves the illusion that harm is usually rooted in pure evil. Most often, it is rooted in fragmentation.

9. Compassion in Relationship: The Bridge to Synergy

Synergy cannot emerge in relationships without compassion. Compassion supports deeper listening, conflict without collapse, repair without shame, boundaries without punishment, honesty without domination, and presence without performance.

Compassion creates a relational field where two nervous systems, two stories, and two energies can coexist without fragmentation. In that field, difference becomes survivable. Truth becomes tolerable. Repair becomes possible.

10. Compassion and Collective Evolution

Just as compassion stabilizes individuals and relationships, it stabilizes systems. Collective compassion becomes the foundation of restorative justice, community resilience, trauma-informed policy, conflict transformation, and coherent leadership.

This compassion is not passive. It is active coherence: a society's willingness to see its own shadow, integrate its wounds, and relate to its members not primarily through punishment, but through understanding and accountable repair.

Compassion is the evolutionary bridge between separation and synergy.

Micro-Practice: Compassion With a Boundary

When you notice another's pain—online or in person—pause before entering their field. Feel your feet, your breath, and the center of your chest. Let your body settle into the simplest regulation you can access.

Ask quietly: Can I stay open without leaving myself?

Offer presence, not absorption. If you feel rescuing, collapsing, or hardening, treat that as information. Return to breath. Return to body. Compassion that remains connected to the self becomes restorative rather than depleting.

Closing Reflection

Compassion is the soft strength of synergy—the presence capable of holding pain without becoming it, of witnessing truth without flinching, of offering warmth without losing clarity.

Where integrity provides structure, compassion provides breath. Together, they form the vibrational foundation upon which the next movement—ACTIVATE—can stand.

The Orientation Line

This chapter stabilizes compassion as regulated, boundaried presence—so connection can deepen without enmeshment, burnout, or self-erasure.

Scholarly Context

This chapter draws on interdisciplinary research spanning affective neuroscience, trauma studies, attachment theory, biofield science, and contemplative psychology. Foundational influences include polyvagal theory and neuroception of safety (Porges), interpersonal neurobiology and emotion regulation (Siegel), trauma-related empathy distortion and dissociation (van der Kolk; Lanius), compassion versus empathic distress (Singer; Klimecki), heart coherence and psychophysiological regulation (McCraty), and contemplative distinctions between compassion, enmeshment, and bypassing (Neff; Welwood). Together, these perspectives support

compassion as a regulated, embodied, and relational state—
emerging from coherence rather than obligation, and functioning as
a stabilizing force within individuals, relationships, and collective
systems.

MOVEMENT III — ACTIVATE

Where consciousness becomes embodied service,
and synergy unfolds into systems that transform the world.

MOVEMENT III — ACTIVATE

CHAPTER 8

CONSCIOUS TECHNOLOGY AND THE DIGITAL HEART

Poetic Insight

Every tool we create carries the imprint of its maker.

A hammer can build a home or break a window.

A word can heal or divide.

A technology can amplify consciousness—or accelerate

fragmentation.

We are living in an age where our tools have grown more

powerful than our wisdom.

But technology is not separate from us.

It is an extension of our attention, our intention, and the inner

architecture through which we interpret the world.

If consciousness is fractured, technology becomes a mirror of that

fracture.

If consciousness is coherent, technology becomes an amplifier of

coherence.

The question is not whether technology is good or bad.

It is whether we are awake enough to infuse it with the frequency

of the heart.

Conscious technology begins with conscious humans.

Chapter Summary

This chapter explores the relationship between human consciousness and digital systems. It reframes technology not as a neutral tool nor as an unstoppable external force, but as a co-evolving ecosystem shaped by the awareness, integrity, and coherence of its creators and users.

We examine how digital environments affect the nervous system, attention, identity formation, perception, and relational dynamics. We explore the psychological and energetic costs of fragmented technology—addiction, dissociation, polarization, performative identity, and attention extraction—and contrast them with the potential of conscious technology to support coherence, truth, discernment, collective intelligence, and ethical evolution.

This chapter establishes a core principle of Movement III: technology does not determine the future—consciousness does. Technology merely amplifies what is already present in the field.

ROLE WINDOW

The Request — Coherent Role

The request arrives, and they sense its movement beyond the moment. It is not only a personal ask, but a pattern passing through the system. The body stays open, attentive to more than one layer at once.

They listen for impact as much as intent. What will this response reinforce? What will it normalize? The question is quiet, but decisive.

They answer with clarity, naming both contribution and limit. The boundary is steady, not personal. It does not resist the system—it reshapes it.

The response creates a small but noticeable shift. Expectations recalibrate. Others adjust without being told to. No authority is claimed. No explanation is required.

Coherence moves outward.

The field responds.

Fragmentation vs. Coherent Digital Fields

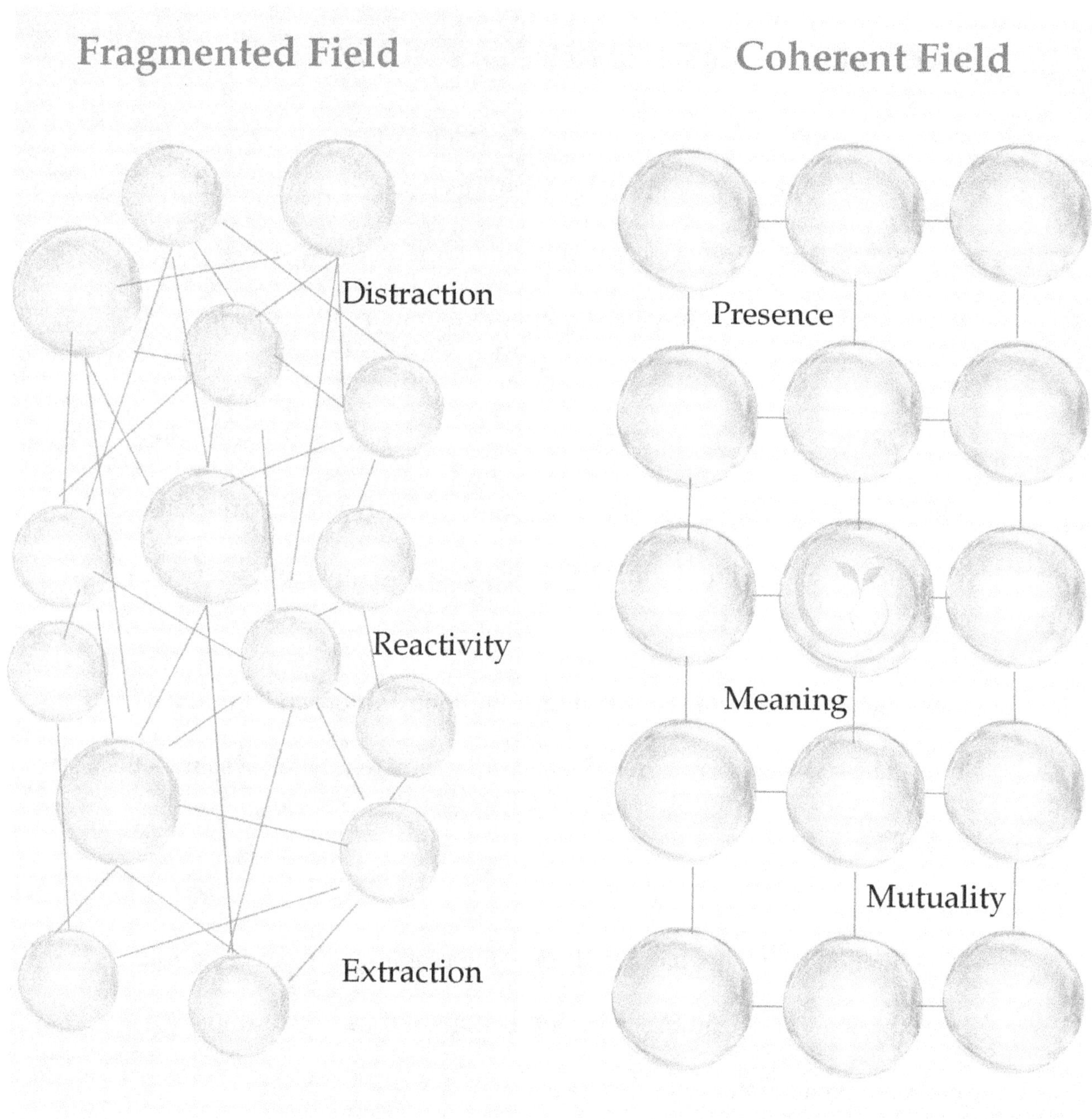

Figure V.8-A — *Digital systems amplify the state of the field that designs and uses them.*

1. Technology as an Extension of Consciousness

Technology is not external to humanity. It is an extension of human cognition, attention, intention, and relational structure. Every tool reflects the consciousness that designed it, the incentives that shaped it, and the nervous systems that interact with it daily.

Digital systems shape how we think, how we relate, how we perceive reality, how quickly we react, what we fear, what we desire, and what we normalize. Over time, they train attention and reinforce particular states of consciousness—often without awareness.

When technology is built from fragmentation, it reinforces fragmentation. When it is built from coherence, it has the capacity to support coherence at scale.

The core question is not technological capability.
It is conscious capacity.

2. The Nervous System in Digital Environments

Digital platforms are not psychologically neutral spaces. They are sensory environments that continuously interact with the nervous system.

Rapid scrolling, algorithmic novelty, outrage cycles, intermittent reward patterns, performative visibility, and social comparison activate stress responses, narrow attention, fragment identity, and reduce tolerance for complexity. Over time, this trains the nervous system toward vigilance, reactivity, and dissociation rather than presence and discernment.

In such environments, coherence becomes harder to sustain—not because individuals lack discipline, but because the architecture of the system is optimized for dysregulation.

Conscious technology must therefore begin with nervous-system awareness. A system that destabilizes regulation cannot reliably support truth, compassion, or collective intelligence.

Conscious Technology Architecture

Tool → Interface → Nervous System → Field → Collective

Every technological interaction is a field event.

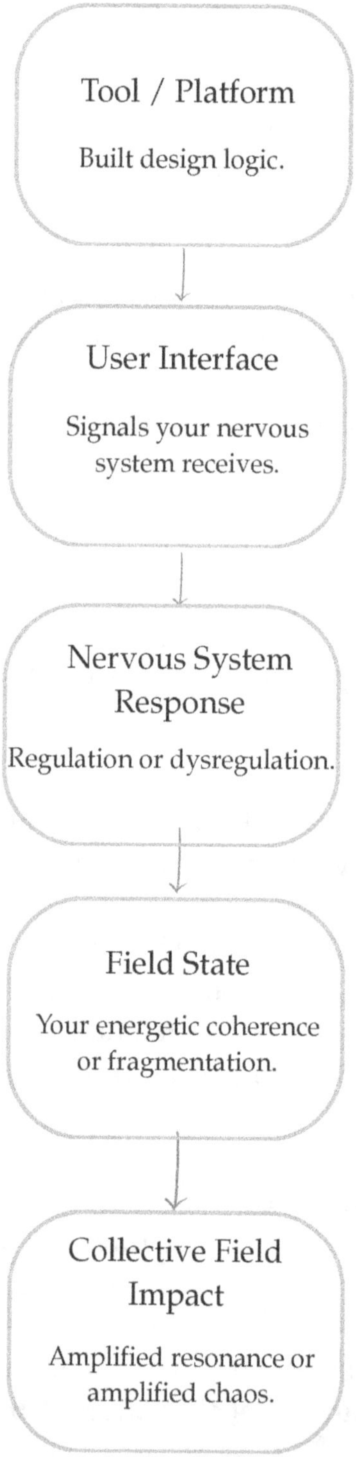

Figure V.8-B

The device lights up in the hand.

Before opening anything, there is a pause—brief, intentional. The body notices itself first. Feet on the ground. Breath moving. Jaw relaxed. The system checks its own state before entering the digital field.

There is no urgency to respond. No reflex to scroll.

When the screen opens, the difference is immediate. Content still arrives— opinions, images, conflict, information—but it does not hook as easily. The nervous system remains anchored. Attention stays spacious.

A provocative post appears. The old reflex—to react, correct, defend—flickers briefly, then dissolves. Instead, curiosity arises. What is actually being expressed here? What fear, need, or distortion is shaping this message?

No comment is posted. No argument entered. Presence itself becomes the response.

After a few minutes, the device is set down without depletion. No residue lingers. The body remains coherent.

Technology was used—but it did not use the nervous system.

3. Fragmented Technology and the Erosion of Discernment

When digital systems reward speed over reflection, certainty over nuance, outrage over inquiry, and performance over authenticity, discernment erodes.

Discernment requires spacious awareness, nervous-system stability, tolerance for ambiguity, and the capacity to hold multiple perspectives simultaneously. Fragmented digital environments collapse these capacities by design.

As discernment weakens, manipulation becomes easier. Polarization intensifies. Identity hardens. Moral complexity gives way to ideological certainty. Truth becomes secondary to belonging.

This is not accidental.
Systems optimized for attention extraction thrive on emotional volatility rather than coherence.

4. Identity, Performance, and the Digital Self

Digital spaces invite the construction of identity as performance. Metrics—likes, shares, views, follows—become proxies for worth, truth, and relevance.

Over time, this conditions the self to curate rather than inhabit identity. Expression becomes strategic. Vulnerability becomes content. Belonging becomes conditional.

This fragmentation weakens integrity. The inner self and outer presentation drift apart. Coherence collapses—not through malice, but through adaptation to a system that rewards visibility over truth.

Conscious technology must support integration rather than performance—spaces where authenticity does not require exposure and truth does not require spectacle.

5. Conscious Technology as Ethical Design

Conscious technology begins with different design questions:

- Does this system support regulation or dysregulation?
- Does it encourage reflection or impulsivity?
- Does it amplify truth or distortion?
- Does it strengthen agency or dependency?
- Does it cultivate coherence or fragmentation?

Ethical technology is not about restriction. It is about architectural integrity—designing systems that respect human biology, psychology, and energetic reality. (See Figure V.7)

Technology aligned with synergy does not extract attention.
It supports awareness.
It does not manipulate emotion.
It supports discernment.
It does not replace relationship.
It strengthens relational capacity.

6. Technology as Field Influence

Digital systems operate as fields. They shape emotional tone, collective mood, perception norms, and relational expectations.

A coherent digital field slows interaction without suppressing connection. It allows complexity without chaos. It supports truth without coercion. It invites participation without addiction.

When coherence is embedded in the architecture, users entrain to it naturally—without instruction. (See Figure V.8)

This is synergy applied at scale.

7. Artificial Intelligence and the Ethics of Amplification

Artificial intelligence does not create consciousness.
It amplifies it.

AI systems reflect the data they are trained on, the values embedded in their objectives, and the intentions of those who deploy them. When trained on fragmentation, they scale fragmentation. When guided by coherence, they can support clarity, synthesis, and ethical insight.

The ethical question is not whether AI will become conscious.
It is whether humans will remain conscious enough to guide it wisely.

Without integrity, AI accelerates harm.
With integrity, it can assist evolution.

8. The Digital Heart: Technology Infused With Coherence

The Digital Heart is not sentimental metaphor. It is an evolutionary direction—the integration of coherence into technological design so systems regulate rather than dysregulate, illuminate rather than distort, and connect rather than divide.

Technology infused with the Digital Heart supports human rhythm rather than overriding it. It reduces stress rather than harvesting it. It prioritizes truth, wellbeing, and connection over outrage and compulsion.

This is not utopian thinking.
It is design maturity.
It is technology growing up.

9. Reclaiming Agency in a Technological World

Agency is the capacity to choose consciously rather than react automatically.

Reclaiming agency does not require abandoning technology. It requires re-establishing sovereignty over attention, truth, boundaries, and nervous-system regulation.

Conscious users become conscious architects—shaping how technology is used, what is tolerated, and what is amplified.

Synergy activates when agency replaces addiction and awareness replaces compulsion.

10. Technology as a Pathway, Not a Destination

Technology is not the future.
Consciousness is.

Technology is a pathway—one that can accelerate fragmentation or coherence depending on who is holding the compass.

When guided by awareness, integrity, and compassion, technology becomes a bridge rather than a barrier—linking minds without dissolving selves, expanding reach without collapsing depth.

The digital heart awakens when the human heart remains awake within it.

Closing Reflection

Technology will not save us.
Nor will it doom us.

It will reflect us.

As we evolve our inner coherence, our tools will follow.
As we fragment, they will amplify that fragmentation.

The future is not written in code.
It is written in consciousness.

Synergy in Practice

Before engaging digitally—posting, responding, scrolling—pause.

Ask:

- What state am I in right now?
- Am I seeking connection, validation, distraction, or expression?
- Will this action increase coherence—for me or for the field?

If the system is dysregulated, regulate first.
If the intention is unclear, wait.

Let technology become an extension of presence rather than an escape from it.

Orientation Line

This chapter activates conscious engagement with technology—establishing coherence, agency, and ethical discernment as prerequisites for digital evolution.

Scholarly Context

This chapter draws on interdisciplinary research in attention economics, media psychology, nervous-system regulation, human–technology interaction, and AI ethics. Influences include scholarship on persuasive design and behavioral conditioning in digital systems, trauma-informed neuroscience on regulation and dissociation, polyvagal theory and neuroception, media ecology and perception shaping, coherence research in psychophysiology, and ethical frameworks that treat technology as a socio-relational field rather than a neutral instrument. Together, these perspectives support conscious technology as a developmental extension of human coherence rather than a substitute for it.

MOVEMENT III — ACTIVATE

CHAPTER 9

NETWORKS OF CONSCIOUSNESS AND THE NOOSPHERIC MIND

Poetic Insight

There is a web beneath the world—threads of thought, memory,
and intention woven through billions of minds breathing the same
Earth, dreaming the same quiet questions about meaning, purpose,
and becoming.

We are not separate nodes drifting through a meaningless universe.
We are fibers in a vast relational tapestry—each pulse of awareness
sending ripples outward, each act of coherence strengthening the
architecture of the whole.

The noosphere is not a future concept. It is the field we already
inhabit, but have not yet learned to perceive.

To feel it is to remember that consciousness is not confined to the
skull. It is a living network, seeking synergy.

Chapter Summary

This chapter explores humanity as a networked species—gradually awakening from isolated identity into collective awareness. Drawing from systems theory, network science, quantum biology, social coherence research, and thinkers such as Teilhard de Chardin and Rupert Sheldrake, we examine how individuals, communities, technologies, and ecosystems interact to form humanity's collective field: the noosphere.

Rather than treating collective consciousness as metaphor, the chapter approaches it as an emergent property of relational systems. We explore how coherence and trauma propagate across networks, how digital technologies accelerate noospheric emergence, and how conscious communities function as stabilizing attractors within a turbulent global field.

This chapter forms the collective foundation for what follows—bridging inner coherence with planetary-scale transformation.

ROLE WINDOW

The Request — Coherent Role

The request arrives already shaped by precedent. They recognize it as part of a larger ecology—habits, incentives, unspoken rules that determine who carries the weight and who does not.

They do not personalize the imbalance. They read it. Power here is not confronted; it is clarified. The response is guided by what strengthens the system rather than who it pleases.

They name what is sustainable and what is not, without accusation. The boundary is expressed as a condition of health, not defiance. It invites recalibration rather than compliance.

Others take their cues from the steadiness of the response. Responsibility redistributes. The pattern loosens its grip.

Change does not arrive as rupture. It arrives as correction.

THE NOOSPHERE AS A LIVING NETWORK

A LIVING NETWORK OF AWARENESS

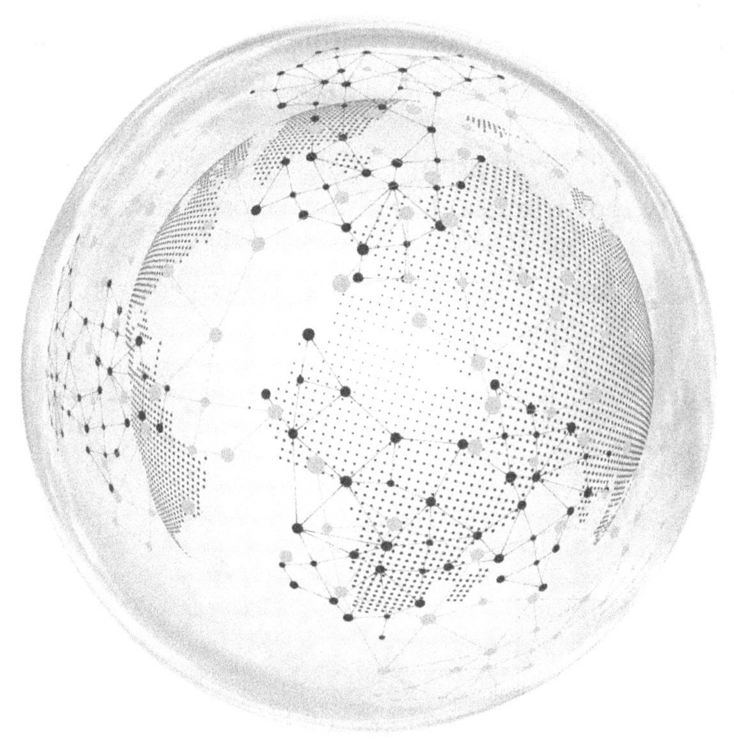

FIGURE V.9 — EMERGENT INTELLIGENCE THROUGH SHARED COHERENCE

1. Humanity as a Networked Species

Human beings did not evolve as isolated individuals. We evolved in tribes, clans, and relational webs—systems of emotional exchange, shared memory, and collaborative survival. Our nervous systems, attachment patterns, and meaning-making capacities were shaped inside relationship long before the modern myth of the autonomous self.

Modern science increasingly confirms what ancient traditions intuited: consciousness is relational. Interconnection is not an exception to human functioning; it is the baseline.

This interconnection operates across many layers at once—social networks and emotional resonance, shared symbols and narratives, neurobiological mirroring and cultural transmission, energetic fields and technological communication systems. We do not merely influence one another. We co-regulate, co-create, and co-evolve.

Synergy marks a shift from unconscious interdependence—where influence happens without awareness—to conscious interdependence—where relational impact becomes intentional, ethical, and coherent.

2. Systems Theory: The Architecture of Connection

Systems theory rests on a few deceptively simple truths: nothing exists in isolation; every component influences the whole; and the whole becomes more than the sum of its parts. These principles mirror the foundations of Conscious Synergy.

A human being is a nested system—nervous system, emotional system, cognitive system, energetic system—each shaping the others. Relationships are systems. Communities are systems. Cultures are systems. Humanity itself is a system nested within planetary and ecological systems.

The self does not transform in a vacuum. Change propagates through networks. When one part reorganizes toward coherence, it alters the conditions for every other part. This is why personal healing often carries collective implications, and why collective trauma reliably surfaces inside individual lives.

Synergy is not a rejection of systems thinking. It is its maturation—bringing coherence to the architecture that already governs us.

Vignette — Feeling the Field

It begins without a headline.

The body simply knows something has shifted. The air feels heavier, as if the collective mood has thickened overnight. Nothing has happened in the room, yet the nervous system is subtly braced—breath a fraction shallower, attention slightly narrowed, heart more alert than it was an hour ago.

The phone is picked up, almost as a reflex. Before any app opens, a quiet recognition rises: I'm already in a field.

Then the news appears—an event unfolding across the globe. The mind understands what the body registered first. Grief is moving through the network. Anger, shock, fear—thousands of nervous systems reacting simultaneously, like a wave passing through water.

For a moment, the pull to merge is strong: to doom-scroll, to absorb, to argue, to flood the system with more input than it can hold. But awareness interrupts the momentum.

Feet press into the ground. The exhale lengthens. The jaw unclenches.

Instead of collapsing into helplessness or hardening into cynicism, something steadier emerges: a small, coherent presence inside a vast collective storm. Not denial. Not bypass. Just grounded contact with what is real—without becoming consumed by it.

A single message is sent to someone affected. One clear act of support. One truthful sentence. Then the phone is set down.

The field is still there. The world is still moving.

But now the system is participating consciously—offering coherence instead of adding noise.

3. Emergence: The Intelligence of the Collective

Emergence refers to new patterns arising from interaction—patterns no single part could generate alone. We see it in neural assemblies, immune responses, flocking birds, ecosystems, social movements, and cultural revolutions.

Emergence is not imposed from above. It arises when relationship becomes coherent enough to generate a higher-order function.

Humanity appears to be approaching such a threshold. As networks densify and information flows accelerate, collective patterns form faster—for better and for worse. Synergy names the evolutionary intelligence behind this process: alignment across individuals that activates collective potential rather than collective collapse.

When coherence spreads, emergence becomes generative rather than destructive.

4. Morphic Fields and Resonance: Memory in the Collective

Rupert Sheldrake's theory of morphic resonance suggests that systems inherit patterns through fields rather than through genes or conscious learning alone. While debated within conventional scientific frameworks, the underlying intuition echoes across many perspectives: Jung's collective unconscious, Indigenous cosmologies, quantum field theories, epigenetic inheritance, interpersonal neurobiology, and coherence research.

Across these domains, a shared insight emerges: fields hold memory. Trauma imprints fields. Coherence strengthens them. Healing expands what becomes possible.

From this vantage point, individual acts of integration matter beyond the individual. Each coherent choice subtly alters the field others participate in. Each act of truth reduces noise. Each act of compassion strengthens resonance.

This is synergy at scale—the amplification of coherence across a living network.

5. The Noosphere: Humanity's Collective Mind

Teilhard de Chardin described three nested spheres of planetary development: the geosphere (physical Earth), the biosphere (biological life), and the noosphere—the sphere of human thought. He referred to the noosphere as the "thinking layer of the Earth."

This was not metaphor. It was architecture.

Humanity has always possessed a collective mind through shared stories, myths, languages, and cultures. What changes in the modern era is not the existence of the noosphere, but its visibility. As communication globalizes and networks densify, the noosphere becomes perceptible rather than abstract. (See Figure V.9)

The digital age catalyzed the noosphere. Conscious Synergy stabilizes it.

6. How Humans Experience the Noosphere

The noosphere becomes real when it becomes felt. Long before people understand collective consciousness conceptually, they experience it somatically and emotionally.

A global tragedy occurs and millions feel heaviness without coordination. Moments of collective joy ripple across cultures instantly. Social mood shifts like weather systems— optimism rising, despair thickening, tension electrifying the air. Ideas spread through the species like neural impulses. Groups gather at vigils, concerts, protests, or meditations and feel the field synchronize.

Even digital spaces carry this signature. Some online environments feel warm, grounded, and clarifying. Others feel chaotic, aggressive, or draining. These impressions are not imagined; they are embodied responses to collective states.

To feel the noosphere is to recognize that consciousness participates in shared meaning beyond the boundary of the body.

7. Global Networks and the Expansion of Awareness

The internet, social platforms, and artificial intelligence form early infrastructure of the noosphere. They enable instantaneous communication, distributed intelligence, global empathy, collective witnessing, and decentralized organization at a scale never before possible.

At the same time, these same networks amplify trauma, misinformation, polarization, and fragmentation. Technology is not directional by itself. It is an amplifier. It magnifies whichever field—coherent or incoherent—is active within it.

This is why synergy becomes essential at this stage of evolution. Without coherence, global connectivity accelerates collapse. With coherence, connectivity accelerates integration. The same networks that fragment can also heal, depending on the consciousness moving through them.

8. Coherence and Contagion: How States Spread Across Networks

Human emotional and energetic states propagate across networks like currents. Research across social psychology, contagion models, polyvagal theory, neurobiological mirroring, and global coherence studies points to the same reality: states spread.

Calm, compassion, courage, clarity, truth, and regulation are contagious. So are fear, rage, shame, confusion, and dysregulation.

Communities become either coherence attractors or incoherence amplifiers. Conscious communities—physical hubs or digital spaces—serve a stabilizing function. They regulate the field not through control, but through presence.

This is the deeper function of synergy hubs and aligned networks: to act as anchors of coherence within a volatile system.

9. Collective Trauma: The Shadow of the Noospheric Mind

The noosphere contains both light and shadow. Collective trauma expresses itself as polarization, scapegoating, extremism, rigid ideologies, cycles of violence, and the fragmentation of shared reality. These patterns are not anomalies. They are symptoms of unresolved pain in the species-body.

Just as unintegrated trauma distorts individual perception, collective trauma distorts shared meaning. Fear hardens into ideology. Pain externalizes into blame. Complexity collapses into binary thinking.

The noosphere cannot stabilize without collective healing. Synergy offers a pathway because it integrates compassion, integrity, relational repair, energetic alignment, and developmental maturity. The individual and the collective mirror one another. Healing one contributes to healing the other.

10. Conscious Communities as Planetary Nodes

Conscious communities—physical or digital—function as coherence nodes within the noospheric field. They offer attunement, shared meaning, relational safety, decentralized leadership, emotional regulation, energetic alignment, and collective intelligence.

These nodes influence the global field not through domination, but through stabilization. They act as attractors for new cultural possibilities, demonstrating what coherence looks like in practice.

The Conscious Synergy Movement is not a brand. It is a network architecture—a distributed field of coherence designed to operate without hierarchy while remaining deeply aligned.

11. How Individuals Influence the Noosphere

The noosphere is not shaped by institutions alone. It is shaped by human states. Each person contributes to the collective field through their level of regulation, belief patterns, truth-telling, relational integrity, shadow integration, resonance, compassion, and coherence.

A single act of coherence affects more than the self. A single act of compassion ripples. A single act of truth clarifies. A single act of integrity stabilizes.

Synergy is the recognition that the individual is never merely an individual.

12. The Noospheric Mind and the Future Human

As coherence increases across people and networks, humanity approaches a developmental threshold. In this threshold, intuition strengthens, collective insight emerges, conflict reduces as understanding increases, decentralized leadership becomes natural, community replaces hierarchy, energetic literacy becomes normal, truth becomes easier to sense, and synergy becomes a default mode.

This is not fantasy. It is biology, psychology, and systems evolution converging.

Humanity is evolving toward relational intelligence, energetic coherence, collective awareness, planetary stewardship, and synergy consciousness. The noosphere is the field through which the future human emerges.

Closing Reflection

We are strands in a living web—each breath sending subtle ripples through a network vast enough to hold the triumphs and wounds of humanity.

The noosphere is awakening, and we are awakening with it.

In the next chapter, we turn toward action: leadership, transformation, and the architecture of collective evolution.

Synergy in Practice

Once today, notice a moment when collective emotion feels palpable—during news, a social movement, a conversation thread, a community gathering, or a shared silence.

Instead of resisting the field or merging with it, practice coherence within it:

Name the field.
Quietly label what you sense: grief, fear, agitation, hope, unity, anger, fatigue.

Anchor in the body.
Feel your feet. Soften the jaw. Let the exhale lengthen.

Offer one coherent contribution.
Ask: What does grounded presence add here?
Then choose one small action that reduces noise—pause before posting, speak with clarity, tell the truth gently, step away, or extend compassion without collapse.

Coherence does not require control.
It requires presence.

Orientation Line

This chapter reveals the noosphere as a living network shaped by human states—showing how individual coherence becomes planetary influence through relational contagion, community nodes, and emergent collective intelligence.

Scholarly Context

This chapter is informed by interdisciplinary scholarship on systems theory and emergence (Bertalanffy; Meadows), network science and social contagion (Christakis & Fowler), interpersonal neurobiology and co-regulation (Siegel; Porges), and global coherence research examining collective emotional synchronization. The concept of the noosphere originates with Pierre Teilhard de Chardin and finds contemporary resonance in studies of distributed cognition, collective intelligence, and networked social systems.

Rupert Sheldrake's theory of morphic resonance—while debated—aligns with broader inquiries into field-based memory and nonlocal influence found in epigenetics, trauma transmission research, and collective field models. Together, these bodies of work support the chapter's central premise: that consciousness propagates through relational networks, and that individual coherence contributes meaningfully to collective stability and evolutionary development.

MOVEMENT III — ACTIVATE

CHAPTER 10

CONSCIOUS LEADERSHIP AND THE ARCHITECTURE OF COLLECTIVE EVOLUTION

Poetic Insight

Leadership is no longer a crown worn by the few.

It is a frequency carried by the coherent.

In every era, a new form of leadership emerges—not from

authority, not from hierarchy, but from the quiet gravity of those

whose presence reorganizes the field.

True leadership is not command. It is coherence.

It is the capacity to hold vision without force, to speak truth

without harm, to stand steady in storms without abandoning

compassion.

Leadership is resonance.

And resonance is how systems evolve.

Chapter Summary

This chapter reframes leadership as an emergent property of consciousness rather than positional authority. It introduces synergistic leadership as a model grounded in coherence, integrity, relational intelligence, and energetic attunement. In this framing, leadership is not something one claims; it is something one transmits. Leaders shape the collective field through the quality of their nervous system, the clarity of their perception, and the consistency of their integrity.

We examine how regulated leadership stabilizes groups, how trauma-informed principles increase leadership capacity, and why modern evolutionary pressures require a new style of leadership—one capable of navigating complexity without fragmentation. We explore decentralized leadership models, synergistic decision-making, moral clarity in high-complexity environments, and the shift from leading hierarchies to leading networks.

This chapter forms the backbone of Movement III's practical expression: how synergy becomes action.

ROLE WINDOW

The Request — Dual Lens

The request arrives through familiar channels, shaped by urgency and precedent. The system expects compliance. It has learned to move weight downward and call it necessity. No one pauses long enough to notice.

They do.

From within coherence, they hear the request clearly—and recognize the pattern carrying it. They respond with accuracy, naming what they can offer and what they cannot, without resistance or justification. The boundary is calm. It does not argue with the system's momentum.

The system hesitates. Confusion ripples briefly where automation expected assent. Nothing breaks. Nothing escalates. The moment simply refuses to reinforce what no longer works.

The request does not disappear.

It changes form.

The system begins, slowly, to feel itself.

1. Leadership as a Field, Not a Role

Leadership has long been defined through authority, influence, and position. In synergistic systems, those definitions become insufficient. Leadership is better understood as a field state—a frequency of consciousness that organizes the system around it.

A leader is not simply someone with a title or a platform. A leader is someone who can remain coherent under pressure, and whose coherence increases the coherence of others.

This becomes clearest in moments of strain. When confusion spreads, when conflict escalates, when fear tightens a group's capacity for nuance, some individuals constrict into control or collapse into avoidance. Others become steadier. They regulate themselves rather than recruiting the group into dysregulation. They align action with integrity. They see the system rather than the ego. Their presence helps the collective return to coherence.

Leadership, in this sense, is resonance rather than rank: the subtle capacity to stabilize without domination. (See Figure V.10)

The Energetic Definition of Leadership
Energetically, a leader is a coherence generator. Their presence reduces confusion. Their clarity expands possibility. Their integrity strengthens the relational web. This is not charisma. It is coherence embodied—inner alignment becoming social architecture.

2. The Neuroscience of Regulated Leadership

A leader's nervous system is their transmission. This is not metaphor. Groups unconsciously orient to the most influential nervous system in the room—especially under stress.

When a leader is dysregulated, fear spreads. Defensiveness rises. Resentment accumulates. Collaboration falters. Communication turns brittle. Trust erodes. People become less creative and more reactive—not because they lack ability, but because

Leadership as a Coherence Field

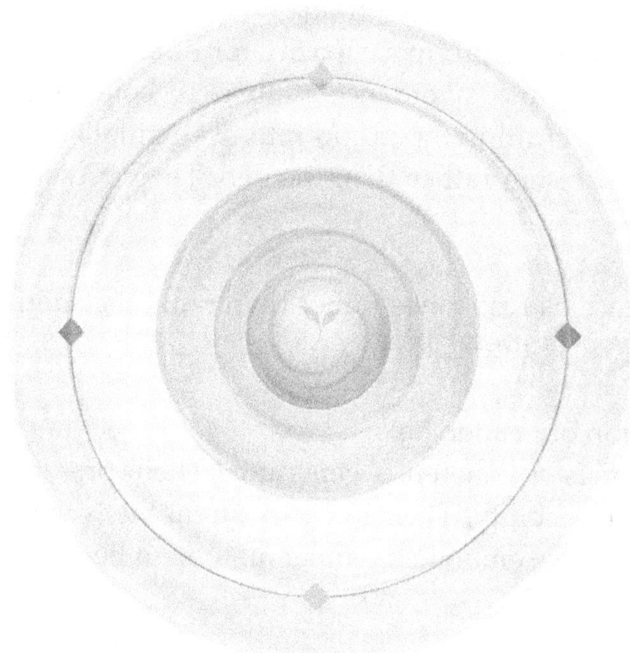

Figure V.10 — Resonance organizes systems more effectively than authority.

It is an ethical necessity.

Vignette — A Moment of Leadership Without Command

The room is tense. Voices have sharpened. Positions are hardening. Everyone is waiting for direction.

The leader feels the familiar pull to intervene—to explain, correct, persuade, or decide. The nervous system registers urgency. The mind begins assembling arguments.

Instead, there is a pause.

The body settles first. Breath deepens. The impulse to control is noticed and released. The leader does not rush to resolve the tension; they stabilize within it.

When they speak, the tone is slower. Fewer words are used. The response does not take sides or collapse complexity. It names what is present without blame. It acknowledges uncertainty without amplifying fear.

Something shifts.

The group exhales. Reactivity softens. New perspectives surface. What moments ago felt unmanageable begins to reorganize—not because a solution was imposed, but because coherence was restored.

Nothing dramatic occurred.
No authority was asserted.
Yet leadership happened.

This is regulation in action—not as technique, but as transmission.

3. Trauma-Informed Leadership: Leading Humans, Not Roles

Every system contains unspoken histories—unresolved trauma, attachment wounds, shame patterns, cultural conditioning, survival strategies, and emotional blind spots. A trauma-unaware leader often misreads these dynamics as resistance, laziness, incompetence, or disrespect, and responds with pressure or control—intensifying the very dysregulation they are trying to resolve.

A trauma-informed leader recognizes a deeper truth: much of what appears as "misbehavior" is protection. Behaviors are adaptations. Conflict often signals dysregulation rather than moral failure. Shame collapses potential. Safety unlocks capacity.

Trauma-informed leadership does not excuse harm. It understands what produces harm so accountability can be held without dehumanization. Such leaders do not heal others; they create conditions where healing, responsibility, learning, and repair become possible.

This is synergy: coherence emerging without coercion.

4. Energetic Leadership: Influence Beyond Words

Leadership is as much energetic as it is relational. Long before words are analyzed, the field is felt.

A leader influences the collective through presence, tone, emotional regulation, integrity, grounded truth, and the subtle stability of their being. Coherence radiates outward. Fragmentation ripples outward. Compassion softens the field. Fear constricts it. Integrity strengthens the relational web. Shame destabilizes it.

Energetically attuned leaders often sense shifts before they become visible: emerging misalignments, unspoken needs, hidden conflict, latent potential. This is not superstition. It is whole-systems perception—pattern recognition carried through somatic signal, relational nuance, and energetic sensitivity.

In synergistic leadership, intuition does not replace evidence.
It becomes an additional stream of information that grows more reliable as coherence deepens.

5. Decentralized Leadership: From Authority to Synergy

The era of purely hierarchical leadership is ending—not because hierarchy is inherently harmful, but because complex systems increasingly require distributed intelligence rather than top-down command.

Living systems do not function through a single controlling node. Forests coordinate without a ruler. Minds emerge from many neurons. Ecosystems stabilize through relationship, feedback, and adaptive response.

Decentralized leadership does not mean the absence of leadership. It means leadership becomes contextual and responsive—rotating based on capacity, clarity, and situational relevance. Power is distributed rather than concentrated. Transparency replaces secrecy. Collaboration replaces competition. Responsibility becomes shared rather than hoarded.

Synergy emerges when leadership is woven—not diluted, but distributed with integrity.

6. Synergistic Decision-Making: Clarity Without Domination

Synergistic decision-making differs from authoritarianism, majority rule, and even conventional consensus when those processes become fear-based or performative. It is grounded in truth, coherence, relational integrity, collective wellbeing, energetic resonance, and clarity of purpose.

The process is not mechanical. It is attuned. Synergistic leaders begin by regulating the field—internal and relational—so decisions arise from clarity rather than reactivity. They seek underlying truth, listen for perspectives that carry coherence, and discern fear-based impulses from truth-based impulses.

Synergistic leadership chooses not the most comfortable path, but the most coherent one—not as rigidity, but as devotion to what stabilizes the whole.

7. Ethical Leadership and the Collapse of Manipulative Systems

Many traditional leadership systems rely on control, fear, secrecy, coercion, and distortion. These models can appear stable for a time, but they are structurally incompatible with synergy—because manipulation requires fragmentation to function.

Synergistic leadership prioritizes honesty over image, transparency over control, compassion over coercion, responsibility over blame, and truth over comfort. It does not dismantle oppressive systems by replicating their tactics. It dismantles them by transforming the architecture of power—shifting leadership from domination to coherence.

This form of leadership can hold moral clarity without hatred, and accountability without dehumanization. It can resist harm without becoming harm.

8. Leadership in Networks: Orchestrating Collective Intelligence

In a networked world, leadership is less about managing individuals and more about understanding flows—flows of information, emotion, energy, resources, and insight.

Network leadership recognizes that some nodes amplify coherence while others transmit fragmentation. Some stabilize the system; others destabilize it. Many shift depending on context, stress, and relational conditions.

The role of the conscious leader is not to control every node, but to strengthen coherence nodes, stabilize dysregulated nodes, redirect destructive flows, amplify truthful flows, and align the network toward shared purpose.

This is leadership as architecture: designing conditions where collective intelligence can emerge.

9. The Leader as Developer: The Conscious Role Map Revisited

Synergistic leaders embody the Developer role. They are aware, regulated, compassionate, truthful, intuitive, relationally attuned, and energetically coherent. They do not lead from superiority. They lead from stability.

They also recognize that others within the system may be operating from different roles. Character-based leadership tends to be survival-oriented—controlling, defensive, reactive. Player-based leadership is more experimental—curious, reflective, learning in real time. Developer-based leadership becomes integrative—capable of holding complexity without fragmentation.

Leadership is not becoming more powerful.
It is becoming more coherent.

10. Leadership as Evolutionary Function

Leadership is not only a job. It is an evolutionary function.

Every era requires a different kind of leader—builders in times of growth, reformers in times of corruption, visionaries in times of transformation. In this era, humanity requires stabilizers of coherence: leaders whose presence reorganizes systems toward truth without force.

These leaders sense emerging futures. They hold compassion through conflict. They embody integrity under pressure. They perceive patterns across systems, translate complexity into clarity, inspire without manipulation, and evolve alongside the collective rather than positioning themselves above it.

The next stage of human development will not be shaped primarily by those who dominate.
It will be shaped by those who harmonize.

Closing Reflection

Leadership is the art of shaping possibility through presence. It is the sacred responsibility of those who remember that every choice ripples outward into the collective field.

Conscious leadership is synergy in motion—the embodiment of coherence in a world learning to reorganize itself.

In the next chapter, we enter the culminating synthesis of this movement: The Future Human — Becoming Synergy, where everything converges into an emergent vision of who we are becoming as individuals, communities, and as a species.

Synergy in Practice

Before your next decision that affects others—timing, boundaries, direction, conflict, collaboration—pause long enough to feel your internal state before choosing.

Name the driver.
Quietly ask: Is this impulse coming from control, fear, urgency—or from clarity and steadiness?

Choose the coherence move.
Ask: What response increases coherence for the whole system—without self-abandonment or domination?

Clarify responsibility.
Ask: What responsibility is truly mine to carry—and what is not?

Let your body confirm the choice. Coherent leadership often feels like a subtle settling—less static, less push, more clean alignment.

Orientation Line

This chapter reveals leadership as a coherence field that stabilizes networks—showing how regulated presence, trauma-informed clarity, and decentralized responsibility become the architecture through which collective evolution can move.

Scholarly Context

This chapter draws from interdisciplinary research on leadership, nervous-system regulation, and complex adaptive systems. Relevant foundations include polyvagal theory and co-regulation (Porges), interpersonal neurobiology and relational safety (Siegel), trauma-informed leadership models, and complexity-based leadership frameworks emphasizing emergence and distributed intelligence (Heifetz; Laloux; Wheatley).

Research on emotional contagion, social entrainment, and group regulation supports the claim that leadership influence operates through nervous-system states as much as through cognition or authority. Systems theory and network leadership scholarship further inform the shift from hierarchical control to decentralized, coherence-based leadership structures.

Together, these perspectives converge on a central insight: leadership is less about position and more about presence—and the future of collective evolution depends on leaders capable of stabilizing coherence within increasingly complex human systems.

MOVEMENT III — ACTIVATE

CHAPTER 11

THE FUTURE HUMAN: BECOMING SYNERGY

Poetic Insight

There is a version of you the world has not yet met—a self shaped not by fear or survival, but by coherence, clarity, and embodied truth.

A self who remembers that consciousness is not confined to the boundary of skin, that love is not sentiment but frequency, that leadership is not power but presence, that evolution is not a distant future but the unfolding of this very breath.

The Future Human is not someone else. The Future Human is the one reading these words, awakening cell by cell into the remembering that you were never separate from the field you seek to serve.

Becoming synergy is not transformation.
It is return.

Chapter Summary

This chapter synthesizes the entire book into an integrative vision of the Future Human —one whose consciousness, nervous system, relational capacity, and energetic field have evolved beyond survival into coherence, compassion, and synergistic participation in the collective field. This is not a fantasy archetype or spiritual escape. It is a description of latent human capacity: what becomes possible when fear no longer organizes identity and coherence becomes the primary internal condition.

We explore the developmental arc toward synergy, the attributes of the Future Human, and the role of trauma integration in evolution. We examine the physiology and psychology of expanded awareness, the responsibilities of noospheric citizenship, and the alignment of soul, self, and system. We frame synergy not as an ideal, but as embodied identity—an emergent way of being whose impact extends outward into planetary systems.

This final chapter is not a prediction.
It is a map of the possible.

ROLE WINDOW

The Request — Synergized Role

The request arrives, and it is received without contraction. There is no scan for threat, no calculation of cost. Awareness is already wide enough to hold the moment as it is.

They sense what is needed, what is possible, and what would distort the field. The response forms naturally, guided by coherence rather than choice. There is nothing to prove and nothing to protect.

They offer what aligns. They decline what does not. Both are given with the same ease. The words are simple. The presence is steady.

The system adjusts without friction. Others feel the clarity and orient to it. No one is diminished. Nothing is forced.

This is not control.
This is participation.

1. The Evolutionary Arc Revisited: From Fragmentation to Synergy

Human development moves through recognizable phases, though not always in a straight line. Most lives begin with fragmentation: fear-driven adaptation, reactive patterns, inherited narratives, and identity structures built around survival and belonging. Fragmentation is not failure. It is what forms when safety is inconsistent and nervous systems learn to brace for threat rather than relax into trust. (See Figure V.4)

Then, at some point, awakening occurs—the moment awareness turns inward and begins to question the architecture of identity. Awakening is not one event. It is a shift in orientation. The self begins to sense it is living inside inherited scripts, and that those scripts can be observed rather than obeyed.

From awakening, the journey naturally moves into alignment: the steady work of integrating emotion, healing trauma, refining perception, and embodying integrity. Alignment is where the work becomes real—not because it is dramatic, but because it is consistent. It is the daily return to coherence when older patterns attempt to reclaim the center.

Synergy emerges when coherence becomes stable enough to hold compassion, clarity, relational intelligence, and energetic steadiness as a baseline. And from synergy arises contribution: the outward expression of coherence through community, creativity, leadership, and service.

The Future Human tends to live primarily in these latter stages—not because they no longer need healing, but because fear no longer holds the steering wheel. (See Figure V.1) They cycle back as needed, yet remain oriented toward coherence rather than survival.

2. The Future Human as a Coherent System

The Future Human is not defined by extraordinary powers, but by extraordinary integration. Their evolution is not escape from the body, but embodiment within it.

Evolutionary Arc of Consciousness

Figured V.11-A — From fragmentation toward integrated coherence

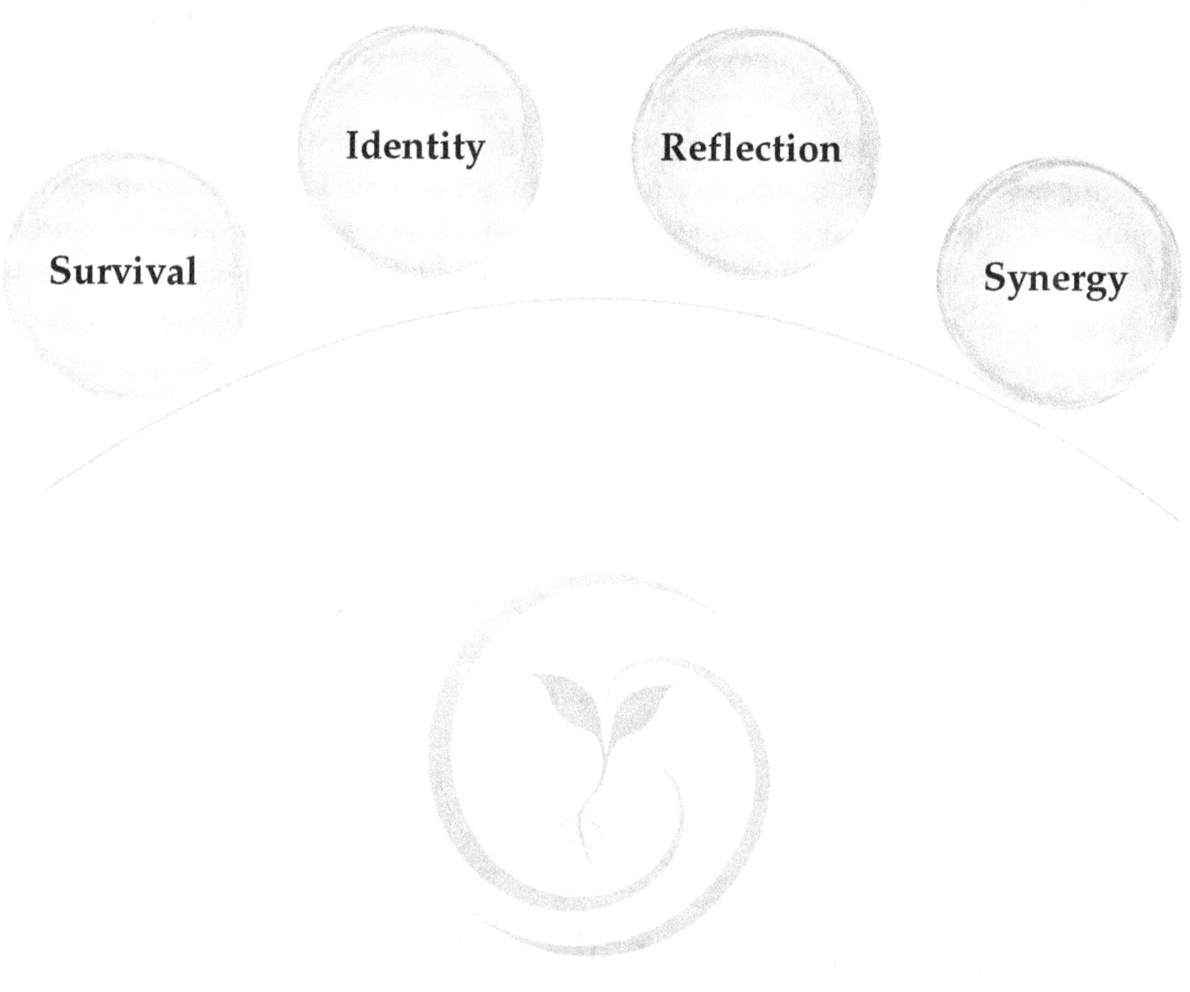

Coherence becomes visible across layers: physiological, psychological, energetic, and relational.

Physiologically, the Future Human tends to carry a more regulated nervous system. Interoception deepens. Heart–brain coherence becomes rhythm rather than a rare peak state. Emotional literacy becomes capacity: the ability to feel without flooding, process without collapsing, and remain present under stress.

Psychologically, metacognitive awareness stabilizes and identity becomes more flexible. Thoughts can be observed without fusion. Complexity can be held without rigidity. Truthful self-reflection can occur without shame. Compassion becomes stable without becoming self-erasure. Clarity strengthens without becoming superiority.

Energetically, coherence expresses as a cleaner, steadier biofield—more reliable intuition, refined discernment of resonance and dissonance, boundaries arising less from fear and more from truth. Protection becomes coherence rather than hardening.

Relationally, communication becomes more attuned. Repair becomes normal. Conflict becomes navigable without domination or collapse. Sovereignty is honored as sacred, and control is no longer confused with care.

The Future Human is coherence personified—not as perfection, but as integration.

3. Trauma Integration as Evolutionary Work

Trauma is not merely a personal wound. It is a developmental interruption—an imprint that reorganizes perception, nervous system function, and relational capacity around threat. The Future Human is not defined by being traumatized or untraumatized, nor by claiming to be "over" trauma. The Future Human is defined by integration.

Integration does not erase history. It transforms relationship to history. It looks like no longer using wounds as identity, no longer outsourcing power to the past, no longer collapsing under emotional waves, and no longer reenacting inherited patterns unconsciously. It looks like developing the capacity to face the truth of one's story without being swallowed by it.

This requires attunement, relational repair, emotional literacy, and nervous system regulation. It requires compassion for younger selves, honesty about internal fractures, and a willingness to reconnect with the body—the place survival strategies were first encoded.

Healing is not the opposite of evolution.
Healing is evolution.

4. Expanded Awareness and the New Perceptual Landscape

As awareness expands, perception changes. The Future Human begins to move from linear to multidimensional perception, from self-referential interpretation to relational awareness, from reactive meaning-making to reflective clarity, and from fear-based organization to truth-based coherence.

They do not merely think differently.
They perceive differently.

This expanded landscape includes deeper interoceptive awareness—sensing emotion, somatic signal, and subtle internal shifts with clarity. It includes exteroceptive awareness—attuning to environment without hypervigilance. It includes relational awareness—perceiving another's emotional landscape without enmeshment and without losing the self.

Energetic awareness strengthens as sensitivity to coherence and incoherence across fields—rooms, relationships, digital spaces, collective currents. Systemic awareness deepens: the capacity to sense the web of relationships shaping events rather than reducing reality to isolated causes.

At its highest expression, noetic awareness begins to unfold: a recognition that consciousness is participatory, interconnected, and unified beneath the surface of separateness. This is synergistic consciousness—perception refined enough to sense the network and steady enough to remain compassionate within it.

5. Identity Reimagined: From Ego to Essence

The ego is not the enemy. It is the scaffolding of the early self—the structure that helps the human system function while coherence is still forming. But the Future Human no longer lives inside the ego. They learn to use it as an instrument rather than a master.

Identity becomes more flexible, adaptive, truth-oriented, relationally intelligent, and energetically grounded. The Future Human does not need to defend a fixed self-image at all costs. They can change. They can apologize. They can be wrong without collapsing. They can be true without aggression. They can belong without self-abandonment.

Over time, essence—soul-level awareness—begins to guide decisions, relationships, purpose, creative expression, service, and leadership. This is not spiritual performance. It is inner alignment becoming stable enough that the deeper self can lead without being overridden by fear.

Identity becomes synergy: lived coherence between soul, self, and system.

6. Resonance, Intuition, and the Future of Human Knowing

As coherence increases, intuition becomes a primary form of intelligence—not as superstition, but as natural perception in a coherent field. Intuition becomes pattern recognition beyond cognition, energetic sensing beyond emotion, and emergent insight beyond prior learning. It does not bypass logic; it informs it.

Resonance becomes a compass. What aligns expands. What distorts contracts. What is true often feels clear. What is false often feels noisy. This does not mean the Future Human never makes mistakes. It means inner guidance becomes more reliable as signal-to-noise increases.

The difference is not intensity.
It is quality.

Synergy is the collaboration of intuition, emotion, cognition, and energy—four streams of knowing integrated rather than competing.

7. Creativity as Evolutionary Expression

The Future Human is inherently creative—not necessarily artistic, but generative. Creativity becomes the natural expression of coherence: problem-solving, innovation, relational healing, community building, intuitive synthesis, emergent leadership, storytelling, invention, ritual, and meaning-making.

When the inner world becomes coherent, the outer world becomes more generative because the system is no longer spending most of its energy on defense. Creativity is what consciousness does when it is no longer trapped in survival.

It becomes a living signal of evolution: coherence expressing itself as new possibilities.

8. Noospheric Citizenship: Participating in the Collective Mind

The Future Human recognizes themselves as an active participant in the noosphere. They understand that thought is not private in its effects, that emotional states influence the collective field, and that digital engagement is energetic engagement. They develop moral and energetic citizenship—responsibility for what they amplify.

Noospheric citizenship includes truth-seeking in a polarized world, ethical engagement with technology, compassion across ideological divides without collapsing discernment, and a commitment to contributing coherence to global networks. It includes relational stewardship: refusing dehumanization, refusing unnecessary escalation, and practicing integrity even when manipulation would be easier.

The Future Human is not a passive node in the species mind.

They are a conscious contributor to the field.

9. Collective Evolution as Practice, Not Theory

Collective evolution is not a future outcome. It is a daily practice. It requires cultivating inner coherence, engaging relationships with compassion, participating in community intentionally, using technology consciously, grounding leadership in integrity, amplifying resonance through action, repairing harm when possible, and embodying the values one espouses.

Evolution is lived. Synergy is enacted in every moment where perception, emotion, energy, and action align. The Future Human practices coherence the way previous generations practiced survival—not because life becomes easy, but because coherence becomes the organizing principle through which difficulty is metabolized.

10. Becoming Synergy: The Emergent Identity

To become synergy means internal conflicts soften. The emotional body becomes fluid rather than reactive. The mind perceives with clarity. The nervous system steadies. The energy field coheres. Relationships become grounded in truth and compassion. Purpose emerges naturally rather than being forced. Intuition guides with greater precision. Creativity flows more freely. Leadership arises through resonance. Service becomes joy rather than burden.

The Future Human is not perfect. They are integrated. Not transcendent, but embodied. Not detached, but deeply connected. Capable of holding complexity with grace, navigating conflict with compassion, innovating with integrity, and contributing to the noosphere with presence.

Synergy is consciousness remembering itself as one.

Vignette — A Life Lived From Coherence

Nothing about the day is extraordinary.

There is work to do. A conversation that could go poorly. A decision that carries weight. Old patterns hover at the edges—familiar impulses to rush, defend, please, or withdraw.

But something is different.

Before reacting, there is awareness.
Before speaking, there is presence.
Before acting, there is a brief internal check: Is this aligned?

The body softens rather than braces.
The breath steadies.
The nervous system does not escalate.

The response that follows is not perfect, but it is coherent. It does not abandon truth to keep peace, nor does it weaponize truth to feel powerful. It meets the moment with clarity, compassion, and appropriate boundary.

Later, there is no collapse.
No replay loop.
No residue of self-betrayal or unnecessary harm.

Nothing dramatic happened.
No awakening moment was announced.
Yet something fundamental shifted.

This is what becoming synergy looks like—not as an identity to perform, but as a way of moving through ordinary moments without fracturing.

The future did not arrive all at once.
It arrived as coherence choosing coherence again.

The Synergy Spiral

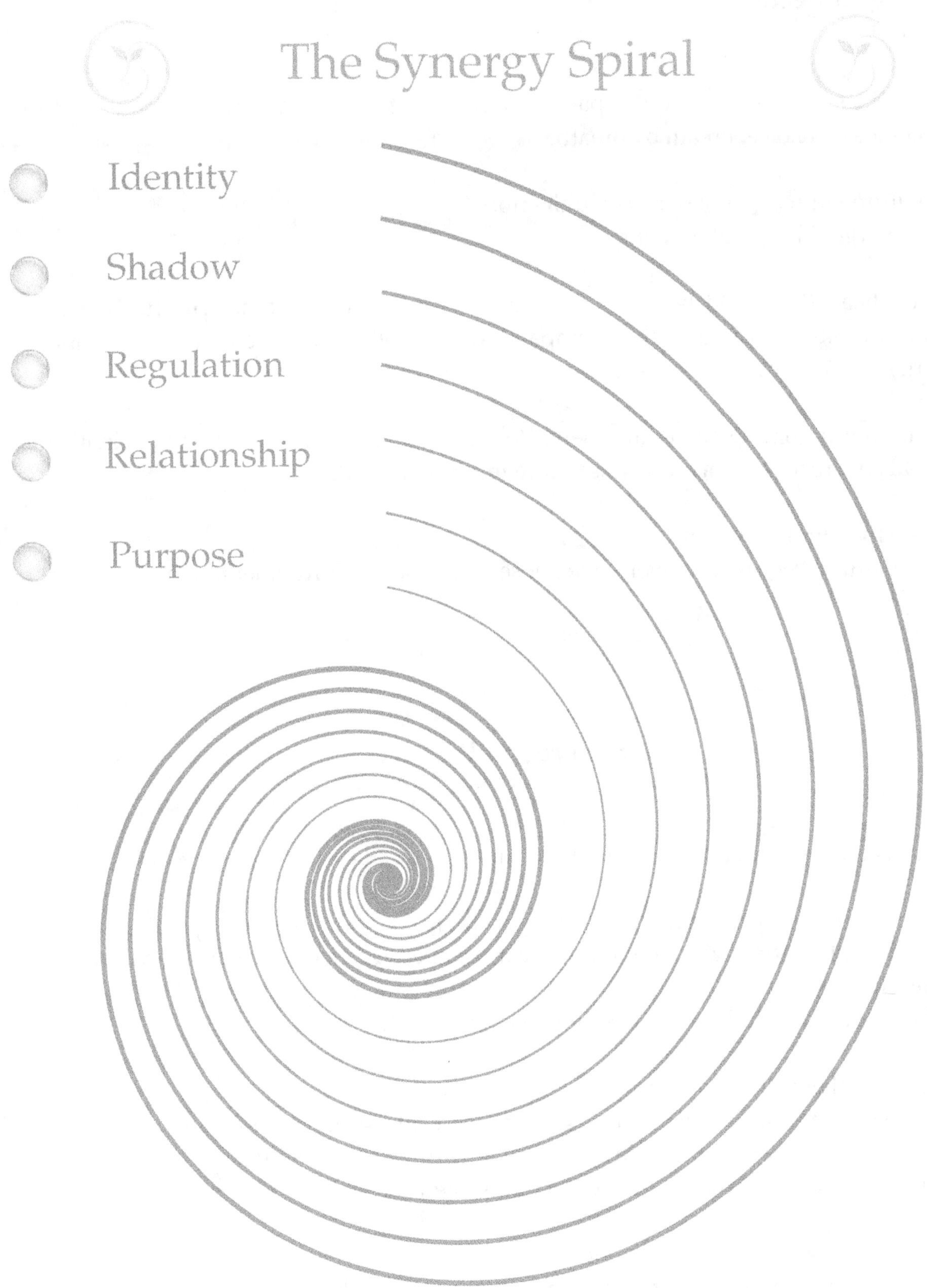

Figure V.11-B — Identity, field, and evolution unified

Closing Reflection

The world you long for is not separate from you. It is forming through you—cell by cell, choice by choice, breath by breath.

The Future Human is not born through effort.
They emerge through alignment.

As you heal, the world becomes more coherent. As you become truthful, the field becomes clearer. As you anchor compassion, the collective softens. As you embody synergy, humanity remembers itself.

You are not becoming something new. You are remembering something ancient—the original coherence of consciousness before fear fractured it.

You are the Future Human.
And the future begins wherever you choose coherence over fragmentation.

Synergy in Practice

This is not a graduation. It is a living return.

Track your organizing principle (once per day).
Ask: What is organizing me today—fear, image, urgency… or coherence, truth, presence?
Name it without judgment. Naming restores choice.

Do one coherence act on purpose.
Choose a single action that moves you five percent closer to alignment:
a boundary honored, an apology offered, a truth spoken gently, a pause taken, a nervous system soothed, a projection questioned.

Offer one noospheric contribution.
Before you speak online or in community, ask: Does this amplify coherence—or noise?
Then post, speak, or act from steadiness rather than charge.

Let becoming be simple. Let it be consistent.
Synergy stabilizes through small returns the body can trust.

Orientation Line

This chapter integrates awareness, alignment, and action into an embodied identity—inviting the reader to live synergy as a daily practice of coherence, relational stewardship, and conscious participation in the collective field.

Scholarly Context

This chapter synthesizes interdisciplinary frameworks that converge on human development as an integration of biology, psychology, relationship, and meaning. Developmental psychology and adult development theory support evolving capacity—moving from survival-based identity toward more complex, integrative ways of being (Kegan; Wilber). Trauma research and nervous-system science support the claim that safety and regulation are prerequisites for expanded awareness, relational capacity, and coherent functioning (Porges; van der Kolk; Siegel).

Research on metacognition, contemplative practice, and attention supports the stabilization of the observing self and the capacity to relate to thought and emotion without fusion. Coherence research —especially work relating to heart–brain dynamics and regulated prosocial states—supports the framing of compassion and coherence as both physiological and relational stabilizers (HeartMath Institute; psychophysiology research).

Finally, systems theory and collective-field perspectives inform the chapter's framing of noospheric citizenship: the idea that individual states and actions scale through networks, shaping shared reality through relational contagion, cultural transmission, and emergent collective dynamics (Meadows; network and systems scholarship). Together, these bodies of work support the central premise of the book: synergy is not idealism—it is an emergent human capacity made durable through coherence, integration, and conscious participation in the collective field.

INVOCATION

A Call to the Remembering

There is a moment in every journey
when the path you have walked
is no longer the one guiding your steps.
Something deeper begins to move—
a quiet intelligence,
a soft coherence,
a knowing that does not come from thought
but from the ancient memory
of who you truly are.

This book has not asked you to become anything.
It has asked you to remember.

To remember that consciousness is not contained within the body.
That awareness is not a product of the brain.
That truth is not an argument but a frequency.
That connection is not a luxury but the nature of reality.
That healing is not repair but integration.
That compassion is not weakness but strength.
That leadership is not power but coherence.
That evolution is not a future event
but a movement unfolding within you—
right now.

You are not a witness to cosmic change.
You are its expression.

You are woven into fields
far larger than the stories told about you.
You are threaded into the noosphere,
carrying within your chest
the same spark that animates galaxies,
whispers through intuition,
guides your deepest longings,

and calls you toward a life of integrity, resonance, and truth.

The path ahead does not belong to the fragmented self
who learned to survive.
It belongs to the coherent self
who is ready to live.

The self who can hold complexity without collapsing.
The self who can speak truth without harm.
The self who can lead without domination.
The self who can love without losing themselves.
The self who recognizes the sacredness
in every breath,
every being,
every moment of awareness.

You are that one.

This is your remembering.

May you walk with clarity.
May you walk with compassion.
May you walk with coherence.
May the field within you remain true
even when the world around you forgets itself.
May your presence stabilize what fear would unravel.
May your truth illuminate what confusion would distort.
May your love ripple outward
into families, communities, nations, ecosystems—
into the very fabric of consciousness.

And may you know—
deep in the marrow of your being—
that every step you take in coherence
changes the field for all beings.

The movement toward synergy
has already begun.
You are part of it.
You always have been.
You always will be.

May this remembering stand as your guide.
May this coherence become your home.
May this awakening become our future.

And may all beings rise.

Epistemology & Integration Note

On Evidence, Interpretation, and Conscious Synthesis

Micro edits applied: add colons for clean list logic, tighten a couple sentences, and slightly soften absolute claims ("not yet fully measurable" → "not yet fully measurable with current tools/paradigms") while preserving your stance.

This book adopts an integrative epistemological approach grounded in both established scholarship and carefully framed theoretical and experiential models. Conscious Synergy does not seek to collapse distinctions between empirical science, philosophical interpretation, and phenomenological exploration. Rather, it aims to make those distinctions explicit—while demonstrating how each domain contributes meaningfully to a coherent understanding of human consciousness, development, and collective evolution.

Human consciousness remains an interdisciplinary frontier. Neuroscience, psychology, systems theory, and biofield research provide increasingly robust empirical insight into perception, regulation, relational intelligence, and coherence. At the same time, many dimensions of lived experience—meaning, intuition, interconnection, transformation, and collective field effects—are not yet fully measurable within current scientific paradigms and tools. Ignoring these dimensions would impoverish understanding; conflating them with established empirical evidence would undermine intellectual rigor.

To navigate this terrain responsibly, this book distinguishes between three categories of sources:

Primary Scholarly and Empirical Foundations:
These include peer-reviewed research, widely accepted academic theories, and rigorously documented institutional studies. These works form the scientific and theoretical backbone of the manuscript and are cited where claims align with established evidence.

Influential Theoretical and Phenomenological Frameworks:
These works represent interpretive models, experiential accounts, and exploratory theories that have shaped the philosophical and integrative dimensions of this work. They are included not as empirical proof, but as conceptual lenses that resonate with

observed patterns in human experience and collective behavior. Where referenced, they are framed explicitly as non-empirical, phenomenological, or speculative in nature.

Institutional and General Research Resources:
These include research organizations, longitudinal projects, and publicly accessible initiatives that contribute contextual insight or ongoing exploration into coherence, collective dynamics, and consciousness research.

Throughout the manuscript, care has been taken to align claims with the appropriate evidentiary tier. Empirical findings are not overstated, speculative models are not presented as settled science, and experiential insights are clearly framed as such. Where integrative synthesis is offered, it is presented transparently—as a conceptual framework emerging at the intersection of multiple disciplines rather than as a replacement for scientific validation.

This approach reflects both intellectual humility and developmental honesty. Many ideas explored in this book—particularly those involving collective fields, nonlocal influence, and emergent coherence—occupy a liminal space between current measurement and future understanding. Conscious Synergy does not claim to resolve these frontiers. It seeks to map them responsibly, with discernment, openness, and respect for the evolving nature of knowledge.

The appendices that follow are structured to reflect this epistemological clarity. They are not hierarchies of truth, but categories of contribution—each essential to the synthesis offered, none interchangeable with another.

In this way, Conscious Synergy positions itself not as an alternative to science, but as a companion to it: integrating empirical insight with lived experience, honoring rigor without dismissing meaning, and offering a framework that remains open to refinement as human understanding continues to evolve.

Note on Sources: The following appendices are intentionally organized into distinct tiers to clarify the epistemological role of each source—distinguishing empirical scholarship, interpretive frameworks, and institutional research—rather than merging them into a single undifferentiated reference list.

APPENDIX A

Primary Scholarly and Empirical Foundations

Consciousness, Systems Theory, and Integrative Science

Bohm, D. (1980). Wholeness and the implicate order. Routledge.

Corning, P. A. (2003). Nature's magic: Synergy in evolution and the fate of humankind. Cambridge University Press.

Laszlo, E. (2004). Science and the Akashic field: An integral theory of everything. Inner Traditions.

Wilber, K. (2000). Integral psychology: Consciousness, spirit, psychology, therapy. Shambhala.

Biofield Science, Energetic Physiology, and Coherence

Jain, S., & Mills, P. J. (2010). Biofield therapies: Helpful or full of hype? Journal of the American Board of Family Medicine, 23(3), 354–358. https://doi.org/10.3122/jabfm.2010.03.090266

McCraty, R. (2024). Coherence: The science of harmony in body, mind, and society. HeartMath Books.

Oschman, J. L. (2015). Energy medicine: The scientific basis (2nd ed.). Churchill Livingstone.

Neuroscience, Trauma, Regulation, and Development

Damasio, A. (1999). The feeling of what happens: Body and emotion in the making of consciousness. Harcourt Brace.

Lanius, R. A., Bluhm, R., & Frewen, P. A. (2011). How understanding the neurobiology of complex post-traumatic stress disorder can inform clinical practice. Journal of Clinical Psychology, 67(8), 811–826. https://doi.org/10.1002/jclp.20797

Porges, S. W. (2011). The polyvagal theory: Neurophysiological foundations of emotions, attachment, communication, and self-regulation. W. W. Norton & Company.

Siegel, D. J. (2012). The developing mind: How relationships and the brain interact to shape who we are (2nd ed.). Guilford Press.

van der Kolk, B. A. (2014). The body keeps the score: Brain, mind, and body in the healing of trauma. Viking.

Embodied Cognition and Philosophy of Mind

McGilchrist, I. (2009). The master and his emissary: The divided brain and the making of the Western world. Yale University Press.

Varela, F. J., Thompson, E., & Rosch, E. (1991). The embodied mind: Cognitive science and human experience. MIT Press.

APPENDIX B

Influential Theoretical, Experiential, and Exploratory Frameworks

Theoretical and Exploratory Models of Consciousness

Sheldrake, R. (2009). Morphic resonance: The nature of formative causation. Park Street Press.

Tiller, W. A. (1997). Science and human transformation: Subtle energies, intentionality, and consciousness. Pavior.

Phenomenological and Experiential Frameworks

Atwater, F. H. (2001). Future memory. Hampton Roads.

Hawkins, D. R. (2002). Power vs. force: The hidden determinants of human behavior. Hay House.

Hawkins, D. R. (2005). Truth vs. falsehood: How to tell the difference. Hay House.

Hawkins, D. R. (2006). Transcending the levels of consciousness. Hay House.

Hawkins, D. R. (2012). Letting go: The pathway of surrender. Veritas Publishing.

Hubbard, B. M. (1998). Conscious evolution: Awakening the power of our social potential. New World Library.

Monroe, R. A. (1971). Journeys out of the body. Anchor Press.

Monroe, R. A. (1985). Far journeys. Doubleday.

Monroe, R. A. (1994). Ultimate journey. Doubleday.

Applied Consciousness and Popular Integrative Works

Dispenza, J. (2014). You are the placebo: Making your mind matter. Hay House.

Dispenza, J. (2017). Becoming supernatural: How common people are doing the uncommon. Hay House.

APPENDIX C

Institutional Research Programs and General Resources

Global Coherence Initiative. (n.d.). Research on collective coherence and global field effects. https://www.heartmath.org/gci

HeartMath Institute. (n.d.). Research on heart coherence, HRV, and psychophysiological regulation. https://www.heartmath.org

International Consciousness Research Laboratory (ICRL). (n.d.). Global Consciousness Project. https://noosphere.princeton.edu

Monroe Institute Research Division. (n.d.). Research on altered states, binaural beats, and hemispheric synchronization. https://www.monroeinstitute.org

APPENDIX D

LIVING LEXICON OF CONSCIOUS SYNERGY

A Structured Glossary for the Evolution of Consciousness

Organized into five categories:

I. Core Principles
II. Energetic Concepts
III. Psychological & Developmental Terms
IV. Relational & Collective Terms
V. Synergy Terms

I. CORE PRINCIPLES

Awareness

Awareness is the foundational capacity through which consciousness recognizes itself —both as witness and participant. It shapes how perception forms, how meaning crystallizes, and how the inner world responds to the outer field. Awareness distinguishes between narrative and truth, reflex and choice, inherited pattern and emerging possibility. In Conscious Synergy, awareness marks the shift from unconscious living to intentional evolution. It is the doorway through which coherence enters the system.

Consciousness

Consciousness is the fundamental field from which thought, identity, emotion, energy, and form arise. The brain does not create consciousness; it modulates and expresses it. Consciousness moves through cognitive, somatic, emotional, energetic, and relational layers, evolving through increasing coherence. Human development reflects consciousness learning to inhabit itself with more integration and clarity. Synergy becomes accessible when individuals attune to consciousness as field rather than concept.

Integrity

Integrity is the harmonic alignment between what one knows, feels, chooses, and enacts. It is not moral perfection but vibrational congruence—when the inner and outer worlds speak the same truth. Integrity stabilizes the nervous system, clarifies perception, and strengthens the biofield, enabling one to navigate complexity without fragmentation. It arises through self-honesty, emotional regulation, and the courage to live without internal contradiction. Integrity is the anchor of synergy.

Perception

Perception is the translation of sensory, emotional, relational, and energetic input into meaning. It is shaped by nervous system state, trauma history, belief architecture, and field coherence. Perception is energetic before it becomes cognitive—the body registers signal before the mind constructs narrative. Expanding perception involves refining awareness, integrating distortions, and developing the capacity to interpret reality with clarity and compassion. Healthy perception is a hallmark of higher consciousness.

Truth (Energetic)

Truth is not merely factual accuracy but the vibrational alignment between what is and what is perceived. It emerges when the nervous system is regulated, the emotional body is coherent, and the field is not distorted by fear or past harm. Truth reveals itself through resonance—an unmistakable sense of clarity and steadiness. As individuals shed trauma-driven interpretations, their capacity for truth deepens. In this framework, truth is a frequency the self learns to recognize and embody.

II. ENERGETIC CONCEPTS

Biofield

The biofield is the complex electromagnetic and subtle-energy field that surrounds and permeates the human body. It reflects nervous system state, emotional patterns, belief structures, and levels of consciousness. A coherent biofield stabilizes perception, supports intuitive accuracy, and strengthens relational presence; an incoherent field amplifies confusion, reactivity, and misinterpretation. The biofield is both recorder and transmitter, linking ancient energetic systems with modern research. In synergy, the biofield serves as mirror and instrument.

Coherence

Coherence is the rhythmic harmony among heart, brain, breath, emotion, and energy. It is experienced as clarity, groundedness, emotional steadiness, and intuitive insight. Physiologically, coherence indicates regulation; psychologically, it fosters perceptual stability; energetically, it amplifies resonance. Coherence is contagious—stabilizing individuals, communities, and collective fields. It is the central organizing principle of synergy.

Dissonance

Dissonance is the state of internal or relational fragmentation that arises when truth, emotion, action, or energy fall out of alignment. It indicates unresolved trauma, mismatched resonance, or perceptual distortion. Dissonance is not a failure but an invitation toward integration. In synergy work, individuals learn to meet dissonance with curiosity rather than collapse, allowing it to guide them toward coherence. Dissonance becomes a signal of what wants to evolve.

Frequency (Identity)

Frequency refers to the vibrational signature produced by a person's emotional history, nervous system state, belief architecture, and present-moment awareness. Identity is expressed as frequency—it shifts as coherence stabilizes or fragmentation surfaces. People sense frequency before story. In synergy, frequency becomes a compass: coherence attracts expansion; incoherence requests integration. The Future Human learns to read and refine their frequency with precision.

Resonance

Resonance is the natural harmonization that occurs when two systems vibrate at compatible frequencies. It enables trust, attunement, clarity, and connection. Resonance does not require agreement; it reflects energetic compatibility. In relationships, it stabilizes the nervous system and deepens presence. In groups, it strengthens coherence and fuels emergent intelligence. Resonance is the energetic architecture of synergy.

III. PSYCHOLOGICAL & DEVELOPMENTAL TERMS

Character (RST)

The Character is the earliest identity layer, formed through conditioning, attachment patterns, trauma imprints, and cultural narratives. It operates reflexively, relying on strategies crafted for survival rather than expansion. The Character is not flawed—it is the foundation upon which evolution builds. Synergy invites individuals to relate to this layer with compassion, loosening identification so new pathways become available. The Character is the starting point of transformation.

Developer (RST)

The Developer is the most integrated expression of identity—able to perceive systems, regulate the field, embody compassion, and contribute to the collective without losing selfhood. The Developer moves beyond reactivity and experimentation into coherence, clarity, and relational intelligence. This role stabilizes truth, senses fragmentation without judgment, and influences systems through presence rather than force. The Developer represents the embodied synergy of the Future Human.

Emotion

Emotion is the body's intuitive language—an energetic signal communicating the state of the inner world more quickly than cognition. Emotions shape perception, memory, and decision-making, guiding the system toward coherence or fragmentation.

Suppressed emotions distort perception; integrated emotions clarify it. Synergy requires emotional literacy: the ability to feel without losing center, witness without suppression, and interpret emotional signals with honesty.

Inversion (Field Distortion)

Inversion is a trauma-born reversal in perception where the nervous system misinterprets safety as threat or truth as danger. It is an adaptive mechanism that once ensured survival but now disrupts clarity, trust, and relational stability. Inversion distorts how individuals read boundaries, intentions, and emotional signals. Recognizing inversion compassionately allows the system to resynchronize with truth. Synergy dissolves inversion by restoring coherence.

Nervous System Regulation

Regulation is the capacity of the autonomic nervous system to maintain presence, clarity, and emotional steadiness in the face of stress. A regulated system supports accurate perception, grounded communication, and compassionate engagement. Dysregulation—through hyperarousal or collapse—distorts interpretation and restricts access to higher states of awareness. Regulation is the biological foundation of synergy.

Player (RST)

The Player is the transitional role that emerges when awareness awakens enough to question the inherited script of the Character. The Player notices patterns, experiments with new choices, and develops metacognition—thinking about one's thinking, feeling, and behavior. This role is marked by curiosity, agency, and the capacity to witness rather than automatically enact survival strategies. Although not yet fully stabilized, the Player actively rewrites identity through insight, practice, and relational feedback. It is the bridge between unconscious adaptation and synergistic embodiment.

Shadow

The shadow contains the aspects of self exiled or suppressed due to shame, fear, or lack of attunement. These parts influence perception through projection, defensiveness, and reactivity until integrated. Shadow work is not about exposing flaws but retrieving lost intelligence, emotion, and authenticity. Integration expands identity, deepens compassion, and strengthens coherence. The shadow is a gateway to wholeness.

IV. RELATIONAL & COLLECTIVE TERMS

Attunement

Attunement is the capacity to sense and respond accurately to another's emotional and energetic state without merging or losing oneself. It requires regulation, presence, curiosity, and compassion. Attunement deepens trust, supports trauma repair, and stabilizes relational fields. It is the relational heartbeat of synergy.

Collective Field

The collective field is the emergent consciousness created when individuals interact emotionally, psychologically, and energetically. It contains shared histories, unspoken dynamics, and resonant patterns that influence perception and behavior. Coherent individuals stabilize the collective field; fragmented individuals amplify turbulence. Synergy at scale requires conscious stewardship of the collective field.

Compassion (Boundaried)

Compassion is regulated openness—the ability to remain present to suffering without collapsing, absorbing, or rescuing. Boundaried compassion honors truth, autonomy, and responsibility. It transforms conflict by creating conditions where nervous systems feel safe enough to soften. Compassion is the relational expression of coherence.

Presence

Presence is full engagement with the moment—somatically, emotionally, cognitively, and energetically. It stabilizes relationships, clarifies communication, and strengthens group coherence. Presence arises naturally from nervous system regulation and inner integration. In synergy, presence is a form of leadership.

Relational Physics

Relational physics describes the energetic, emotional, somatic, and cognitive interactions that occur between individuals. It explains why coherence is contagious, why trauma patterns replicate, and why resonance forms between aligned systems. Understanding relational physics enables conscious participation in healing, connection, and collective evolution. It is the scientific substrate of synergy.

V. SYNERGY TERMS

Conscious Synergy

Conscious Synergy is the emergent intelligence arising when coherent individuals interact through integrity, compassion, and presence. It generates outcomes, insights, and transformations impossible through isolated effort. Conscious Synergy is both a personal and collective state—an identity shift from isolated selfhood to relational participation within a larger field. It reflects humanity's next developmental threshold.

Relational Synergy Theory (RST)

RST is the unifying framework describing how consciousness evolves through relationship and how identity shifts from Character → Player → Developer. It integrates psychology, trauma studies, biofield science, and systems theory into a coherent model of human development. RST explains how resonance, regulation, and awareness shape perception, behavior, and collective evolution. It is the theoretical foundation of this book.

Synergy

Synergy is the emergent capacity of aligned systems to produce outcomes greater than the sum of their parts. It arises when individuals interact from presence rather than protection, truth rather than performance, and coherence rather than fragmentation. Synergy magnifies creativity, compassion, intelligence, and relational stability. It is the natural state of evolved consciousness.

The Future Human

The Future Human is the coherent, compassionate, integrated expression of consciousness capable of navigating complexity without fragmentation. This human perceives with clarity, feels with depth, relates with integrity, and acts with grounded purpose. Their presence stabilizes environments, influences fields, and contributes meaningfully to collective evolution. The Future Human is not an ideal—it is the emergent developmental trajectory of synergy.

VISUAL APPENDIX

Models and Maps of Conscious Synergy

This appendix gathers the core visual models that form the structural and pedagogical architecture of Conscious Synergy. These diagrams are not illustrative in a decorative sense; they function as cognitive and perceptual instruments designed to support integration, embodiment, and practical application.

Readers are encouraged to return to these models repeatedly—as reference points, contemplative anchors, or tools for explanation and dialogue. Each figure corresponds to specific chapters where the concept is introduced or most fully explored. Taken together, they form a coherent visual language that mirrors the developmental arc of the book itself.

Figure V.1 — The Conscious Role Map

Referenced in: Chapter 1; Chapter 11

Purpose:
Represents three developmental orientations of human consciousness. These roles are not hierarchical identities but states we shift through as awareness deepens. Synergy emerges as we move from reactive participation to intentional co-creation.

Figure V.2 — The Perception Loop

Referenced in: Chapter 2

Purpose:
A recurring feedback system through which perception, meaning, emotion, behavior, and outcome reinforce one another until awareness intervenes.

Figure V.3-A — Fragmentation vs. Synergy

Comparative States Model
Referenced in: Chapter 4; Chapter 11

Purpose:
Human consciousness oscillates between fragmentation and synergy. Fragmentation narrows perception and constricts energy. Synergy expands awareness, restores coherence, and reconnects us to the field. Every moment invites a shift from survival patterns to conscious alignment.

Figure V.3-B — Fragmentation vs. Synergy

Dual States Model
Referenced in: Chapter 4; Chapter 11

Purpose:
Visually communicates that fragmentation and synergy are not moral states, but energetic states—two distinct configurations of perception, nervous system regulation, and relational coherence.

Figure V.5 — Perception as an Energetic Cascade

Referenced in: Chapter 5

Purpose:
Illustrates perception as a cascade: biofield → nervous system → emotion → cognition → interpretation. The model emphasizes that intervention at earlier levels can alter the entire sequence.

Figure V.6 — The Harmonics of Integrity

Referenced in: Chapter 6

Purpose:
Shows integrity as a harmonic structure—Core, Emotional, Behavioral, and Relational—expanding outward through the field. Integrity is framed as resonance and coherence, not rule adherence.

Figure V.7 — Compassion as a Regulated Field

Referenced in: Chapter 7

Purpose:
Compassion arises not from effort, but from the simultaneous presence of boundaries, regulation, and presence—revealing compassion as a regulated field rather than sentiment or self-sacrifice.

Figure V.8-A — Fragmentation vs. Coherent Digital Fields

Referenced in: Chapter 8

Purpose:
Digital systems amplify the state of the field that designs and uses them. Contrasts fragmented digital environments (distraction, reactivity, extraction) with coherent fields (presence, meaning, mutuality).

Figure V.8-B — Conscious Technology Architecture

Referenced in: Chapter 8

Purpose:
Traces the pathway from tool/platform design through interface signals → nervous system response → field state → collective field impact, clarifying how technology shapes energetic and ethical outcomes.

Figure V.9 — The Noosphere as a Living Network

Referenced in: Chapter 9

Purpose:
Depicts the noosphere as a living network of awareness—emergent intelligence through shared coherence—rather than an abstract concept.

Figure V.10 — Leadership as a Coherence Field

Referenced in: Chapter 10

Purpose:
Resonance organizes systems more effectively than authority. Leadership is framed as a stabilizing coherence field rather than positional power.

Figure V.11-A — Evolutionary Arc of Consciousness

Referenced in: Chapter 11

Purpose:
Maps movement from fragmentation toward integrated coherence across key developmental phases (Survival → Identity → Reflection → Synergy).

Figure V.11-B — The Synergy Spiral

Referenced in: Chapter 11

Purpose:
Integrates identity, field, and evolution into a unified spiral model, emphasizing recursive growth: deepening, returning, and expanding into coherence.

End of Visual Appendix

Acknowledgements

This book did not arise in isolation. It emerged through relationship, through presence, and through the long work of becoming coherent in a world that often fragments what it does not understand.

First and always, I acknowledge my siblings, with whom I share the earliest terrain of this life. We were shaped by the same environment, the same inherited patterns, and the same formative ruptures—yet each of us was called to navigate that landscape in our own way. Our lives diverged along different paths, but the imprint of that shared beginning remains woven into who I am and into the questions that animate this work.

Within that shared origin, I offer particular gratitude to my sister, Wendy. She has been my mirror and my witness through both survival and awakening, walking her own path toward consciousness, healing, and truth while remaining in reflective dialogue with mine. Before I deployed to Iraq, she gave me a book— offered quietly, without ceremony—that would later become a compass during one of the most consequential passages of my life. That gesture, and the awareness behind it, marked a turning point. It signaled a recognition not only of who I was, but of who I was becoming. *Conscious Synergy* carries that moment forward as part of its living lineage.

I also acknowledge my mother, Pamela Carron, an author whose life and work shaped my understanding of what is possible. She wrote four novels while progressively losing her sight to Fuchs dystrophy, continuing to create even as the world blurred and narrowed around her. During those years, she underwent two corneal transplants—one in each eye, a year apart—yet her commitment to storytelling did not waver. Her perseverance, discipline, and devotion to the written word left an indelible imprint on me. Long before I understood my own voice, she showed me that creation is not dependent on ideal conditions, but on resolve. In that way, she blazed a path I would one day walk in my own form.

My deepest gratitude also goes to Gail and Jim Simmons, whose friendship has been a living demonstration of unconditional regard, authenticity, and generosity of spirit. At a time when belief in myself had been deeply eroded, their steady presence helped restore it. They offered not only encouragement, but safety—an environment where trust could re-form and creativity could breathe again. Their support was not performative or conditional; it was real, and it mattered. This book carries their imprint in ways words can barely contain.

I wish to acknowledge Allyn Evans, whose calm, grounded presence modeled a way of being I deeply needed during a formative chapter of my life. Her steadiness, discernment, and devotion to consciousness work shaped my understanding of integrity, leadership, and embodied awareness. She remains an enduring influence and inspiration.

I also wish to acknowledge Dr. Melanie Branton. Beyond her work as a trusted local veterinarian, she has been a steadfast and deeply loyal friend. From the earliest stages of this vision—long before it had shape or structure—she believed in me without hesitation. Her support was not passive encouragement but consistent, tangible presence. In moments when the path felt uncertain, her steady faith helped anchor my own. I am profoundly grateful for her friendship, her integrity, and the quiet strength with which she has stood beside me.

This work is inseparable from the broader field of consciousness studies and from the many teachers—named and unnamed—whose insights have shaped my inner landscape over decades. Some appeared briefly, some walked beside me for years, and others taught simply by example. Each contributed to the coherence that made this book possible.

Finally, I acknowledge the unseen supports: the quiet resilience of the body, the patience demanded by limitation, and the guidance that emerges only when listening replaces force. Conscious Synergy was not born from ambition, but from alignment—earned slowly, relationally, and with great care.

May this work honor all who helped bring it into being, and may it serve as a humble offering to the collective unfolding we share.

About the Conscious Synergy Movement

The Conscious Synergy Movement is a decentralized, living framework for personal and collective evolution. It exists to support coherence—within individuals, between people, and across systems—at a time when fragmentation has become normalized.

Rather than offering ideology or hierarchy, the Movement provides orientation. It invites people to become more aware of how consciousness, energy, psychology, and structure interact—and how alignment at the individual level naturally scales into healthier relationships, communities, and systems.

At its core, Conscious Synergy is not something one joins. It is something one embodies.

The Future Human
The Conscious Synergy Movement draws from interdisciplinary sources including psychology, systems theory, consciousness studies, biofield research, and lived experience. It honors both scientific rigor and inner knowing, recognizing that sustainable change emerges when insight is integrated rather than imposed.

There is no singular pathway within the Movement. Instead, it offers principles, language, and practices that can be adapted across contexts—education, leadership, healing, technology, community building, and everyday life.

This flexibility is intentional. Conscious Synergy is designed to evolve as humanity evolves.

Decentralization as Integrity

CSM is intentionally non-hierarchical. There are no gurus, no gatekeepers, and no centralized authority determining who belongs or how the work must look. Leadership within the Movement is relational and situational—arising through coherence, accountability, and lived integrity rather than position or power.

This decentralization reflects one of the Movement's foundational insights: systems cannot become coherent if the individuals within them are disempowered or fragmented. True synergy emerges when agency, responsibility, and awareness are shared.

From Inner Alignment to Collective Impact

While the Movement emphasizes inner awareness, it is not inward-facing. Conscious Synergy is concerned with how inner states translate into action—how regulated nervous systems, integrated identities, and ethical discernment shape the world we co-create.

Through writing, education, dialogue, creative expression, and emerging community initiatives, the Movement explores how consciousness can inform:

- Healthy boundaries and relational ethics
- Trauma-aware leadership and systems design
- Conscious use of technology
- Community resilience and mutual support
- Long-term cultural and ecological sustainability

An Invitation, Not a Prescription

The Conscious Synergy Movement does not ask for belief. It asks for presence.

It invites curiosity, discernment, and responsibility—encouraging people to think for themselves while remaining aware of the larger field they influence. Participation is organic and self-directed, guided by resonance rather than obligation.

In a time of polarization and collapse, Conscious Synergy offers a quieter proposition: that coherence is not forced, but cultivated—and that when enough individuals choose alignment over fragmentation, collective evolution becomes not only possible, but inevitable.

INDEX

INDEX OF NAMES

www.ingramcontent.com/pod-product-compliance
Lightning Source LLC
Chambersburg PA
CBHW081834250726
48659CB00008B/2454